BASIC BOAT MAINTENANCE

J. Frank Brumbaugh

Bristol Fashion Publications
Rockledge, Florida

Basic Boat Maintenance - - *J. Frank Brumbaugh*

Published by Bristol Fashion Publications

Copyright © 2000 by J. Frank Brumbaugh. All rights reserved.

No part of this book may be reproduced or used in any form or by any means-graphic, electronic, mechanical, including photocopying, recording, taping or information storage and retrieval systems-without written permission of the publisher.

BRISTOL FASHION PUBLICATIONS AND THE AUTHOR HAVE MADE EVERY EFFORT TO INSURE THE ACCURACY OF THE INFORMATION PROVIDED IN THIS BOOK BUT ASSUMES NO LIABILITY WHATSOEVER FOR SAID INFORMATION OR THE CONSEQUENCES OF USING THE INFORMATION PROVIDED IN THIS BOOK.

ISBN: 1-892216-23-X
LCCN: 00-131359

Contribution acknowledgments

Inside Graphics: By the author.
Cover Design: John P. Kaufman

REVIEWS

Good Old Boat - Ted Duke

Basic Boat Maintenance would be a valuable addition to any boat owner's library.

Basic Boat Maintenance - - J. Frank Brumbaugh

DEDICATION

For Mrs. Bernice Pemstein Sanchez, an exceptional woman and my dearest friend for many years. It is a privilege to know her. And also for the skippers and crews of all the small ships wandering the world's oceans, but especially those who go sailing "on a shoestring." This book is for them.

ACKNOWLEDGMENTS

I wish to express my sincere appreciation to the many friendly skippers who gave freely of their time and knowledge while this book was in preparation. They are too numerous to mention here but they know who they are. To each of them, a hearty "Thank you."

I am also indebted to Captain Bob Miller of the fishing vessel *Miss Rose* out of Tampa, Florida, for the opportunity to sail with him as Mate. I learned firsthand the intricacies of diesel engines and the maintenance problems of commercial boats. Thanks, Bob.

Basic Boat Maintenance - - J. Frank Brumbaugh

TABLE OF CONTENTS

INTRODUCTION   Page 9

CHAPTER ONE   Page 13
    Preventive Maintenance Tables

CHAPTER TWO   Page 29
    Hull and Topside

CHAPTER THREE   Page 39
    Sails, Rigging, and Ground Tackle

CHAPTER FOUR   Page 63
    Electrical System

CHAPTER FIVE   Page 75
    Galley, Head, and Plumbing

CHAPTER SIX   Page 91
    Below Decks, Furnishings, and Spares

CHAPTER SEVEN   Page 107
    Instruments and Electronics

CHAPTER EIGHT   Page 117
    Bilge Water and Leaks

CHAPTER NINE *Engines*	Page 129
CHAPTER TEN *Rodents and Insects*	Page 145
APPENDIX ONE *List of Figures*	Page 155
APPENDIX TWO *List of Tables*	Page 157
APPENDIX THREE *Tools & Supplies*	Page 158
APPENDIX FOUR *Glossary*	Page 168
About the Author	Page 189

INTRODUCTION

There is always something which needs doing on a boat. No boat owner will dispute the truth of that statement. Some of these jobs must be done right away; others can safely be postponed, but not forgotten. This book is written to sort out the things which need doing, to place them in proper perspective, and to indicate the simplest and easiest ways of accomplishing what has to be done.

If the little things are done while they are still little, they will never become big. Small discrepancies, not important in themselves, can combine to produce a dangerous situation later, or one which will be expensive to eliminate. Big jobs are more difficult and time consuming than all the small ones which cause them. No boat owner will dispute the truth of that statement.

The boat owner who keeps his eyes open will readily note areas which require attention. He can thus schedule his time so these can be attended to without affecting the use or enjoyment of his boat. Most small jobs can be tucked into spare moments at the dock, and many can be done while under way. Big jobs will be rare, and these can usually be anticipated: Bottom painting and engine overhaul are typical examples.

There are no mechanics or repair shops at sea. All knowledge, tools, and materials available are those aboard the boat. It is up to the boat owner to see all materials and tools which may be required are on board. This book provides much of the knowledge and guidance necessary.

The secret of effective boat maintenance is control. This is best affected by a semiformal schedule of inspection, regularly applied and adhered to. It need take little time or effort, but it must not be neglected lest a little job, unnoticed, grow into a big one. A check list should be used so nothing is forgotten. It will pay to note in the ship's log when an inspection is made as well as a listing of discrepancies noted requiring attention.

Engine hour logs and battery logs, if properly kept, will serve as an excellent reminder and usually give warning before trouble can develop. A preventive maintenance check list such as that given in Chapter One should be prepared for each boat, and individualized to include equipment on board. All boats have hulls, most have engines, many have sails, and some have such extras as a generator and electronic equipment of many kinds. Since no two boats are exactly alike (different boat, different long splice!) your checklist must be individualized for your particular boat.

This book departs from the limited scope of other similar books in that the author's definition of boat maintenance includes the maintenance of safety, convenience, and healthful conditions for all aboard. Thus this book is not limited entirely to the mechanical aspects of maintenance but forges beyond these limitations as necessary.

I have tried to foresee every possible thing which could possibly go wrong on every type of small boat under all possible conditions. It is unlikely I have succeeded but probable that I have come very close. Not everyone will need all the information contained in this book. A few may need specialized information which is outside its scope. But 99 percent of small boat owners will find here all of the general guidance they need to maintain their boats shipshape and in Bristol fashion -- safe, convenient and healthy.

In a few instances I have mentioned certain products by brand name, because they have proven effective and they have been recommended by other sailors and skippers. I want to stress there are other products which are equally effective and may even be better in some instances. The fact I have mentioned brand names does not mean only these products should be used. I have no connection with the manufacturers of any product mentioned by brand name, nor do I receive any remuneration for such mention.

J. Frank Brumbaugh

CHAPTER ONE
PREVENTIVE MAINTENANCE TABLES

Preventive maintenance means a semiformal schedule of minor maintenance performed at regular intervals. This prevents accidental breakdown or warns of its impending occurrence early enough that it may be avoided. It is the least costly but also the most important maintenance for the boat owner.

The simplest program, adapted from one used extensively by the Armed Forces, is called *FITCAL*. This is an acronym formed by the initial letters of six descriptive words; *Feel, Inspect, Tighten, Calibrate, Adjust, Lubricate.* Memorizing this acronym makes it easy to remember the six actions required in this simplest maintenance program. *FITCAL* is briefly described below as applied to small boat preventive maintenance.

Feel -- Use your hands to check for looseness, abrasion, broken parts, overheating, etc.

Inspect -- Visually inspect the boat, her rigging, equipment, etc.

Tighten -- Tighten loose bolts and screws, turnbuckles, etc.

Calibrate -- Check operation of the compass

against its deviation table. Check depth sounder operation against the hand lead line. Using methods detailed in instruction sheets for equipment, calibrate each as required when this is possible.

Adjust -- Adjust as required: Turnbuckles, carburetor, lines, etc.

Lubricate -- Oil moving parts of blocks, pulleys, genoa cars, tracks, pumps, fans, blowers, motors, generators, engines, alternators, rudder pintles, steering gear, hatch slides and hinges, etc.

FITCAL can be applied at any time you are on board and will be a useful adjunct to the more detailed and formal maintenance schedule described in Tables 1 through 4. This formal preventive maintenance schedule has been divided logically into daily, weekly, monthly, and annual or special conditions periods. Those scheduled for daily attention are for times when you are at sea on an extended cruise. They can be safely lumped with the weekly schedule when you are docked or at anchor for long periods. Other scheduled maintenance should be accomplished at the periods given.

Certain preventive maintenance actions are common to many areas of your boat and are mentioned here to prevent the preventive maintenance tables from becoming repetitious.

When checking any electrical equipment make sure it is connected to its power source. Check fuses and replace if blown. If the second fuse blows, remove power and check wiring for short circuits. Replace defective wiring.

When checking plumbing make sure seacocks are open on both intake and overboard drain. If manual pumps do not operate, check O-rings or impellers and replace if required. This also applies to electrically operated pumps after you have made sure of the electrical connections.

Basic Boat Maintenance - - J. Frank Brumbaugh

Tighten, repair, or replace loose, damaged, or missing parts on all mechanical equipment, rigging, etc. Remove corrosion wherever found. Lightly oil all wire cables. Wash antenna insulators often with fresh water to remove salt deposits, but do not oil them. A thin coating of silicone grease may be applied to insulators to prevent rain or spray from bridging them and shorting the antenna out.

Operate all seacocks at weekly intervals to make certain they are operable and to keep them in good condition. Do not leave seacocks open when at sea if the pump outlet is below the water line, except when using them. This applies particularly to the standard marine head on sail boats.

Refer to the instruction manuals for each item of equipment on board for specific maintenance instructions which are beyond the scope of this book. Be sure to follow the manufacturer's instructions for the type of lubricant and the interval for lubricating moving parts. Use only cleansing agents and paints recommended by the manufacturer to prevent damage to the boat or her equipment.

The preventive maintenance procedures of Tables 1 through 4 include not only the boat itself but all equipment and stores normally on board. These procedures should be followed as scheduled, although some may be skipped occasionally by the skipper who is watchful and thoroughly knows the condition of his boat. Not all procedures apply to all boats. Sailboats do not normally have windshield wipers and not every small boat is equipped with a shower. Use those portions of Tables 1 through 4 which apply to your particular boat and ignore the rest.

Battery and Engine Logs, suggested in Table 1, are illustrated in Figures 1 and 2.

Basic Boat Maintenance - - J. Frank Brumbaugh

TABLE 1
DAILY PREVENTIVE MAINTENANCE

DAILY	INSPECT FOR	ACTION REQUIRED
Compass	Operation	Free card. Swings normally. No bubbles. See compass instruction manual for maintenance data.
Sextant	Operation	Check error before use against card in sextant case. Operation should be smooth. If dropped, do not use until checked by repair facility.
Running lights; anchor light; spreader lights; spotlight; cabin lights.	Operation	Bulbs should light when turned on. Replace burned out bulbs. Check fuses if lights are inoperable. Replace blown fuses. If new fuse blows, locate short circuit and repair of replace defective wiring.
Horn, whistle.	Operation	Should operate normally. Replace blown fuse. Repair or replace horn, whistle, or wiring if defective.
Fuel Vapor Detector.	Operation	Needle should jump slightly whn activated even if a safe bilge atmosphere exists. Refer to instruction manual for troubleshooting and repair data.
Blowers	Operation	Blowers can usually be heard. Operation and outflow of air felt. If not operating when turned on, check fuses; replace if blown. If second fuse blows, locate short circuit and repair. Repair or replace defective wiring. Lubricate blower bearings if necessary but do not overlubricate. Replace blower if defective.
Hatches, Doors.	Operation	Should operate smoothly. Lubricate slides and hinges if required.
Rudder, tiller, steering gear.	Operation	Should operate smoothly without binding or noise. Adjust or lubricate as required.
Sails, covers, bags, awnings, dodgers, wind sails, all other canvas products.	Holes, tears, open seams, mildew.	Seams should be tight; no holes or tears. Repair if required as soon as damage is noted.
Windshield wipers.	Operation	Should operate smoothly. Check fuse and replace if necessary. If second fuse blows, locate short circuit and repair or replace defective wiring. If vacuum type, check hoses and connections for leaks or stoppage. Replace as required.

TABLE 1
DAILY PREVENTIVE MAINTENANCE

DAILY	INSPECT FOR	ACTION REQUIRED
Stove	Operation Priming Fuel Leaks	Priming and operation should be normal. If difficulty persists, check fuel for water and if proper type. Replace or clean generator. Be certain valves and fuel line between tank and stove are open and do not leak.
Icebox; drain	Cleanliness, lack of odor	Wash interior with solution of 2 teaspoons baking soda in 1 quart of fresh water. Wipe up spillage. If box not in use prop door or lid slightly open for ventilation. A cup of used, dry coffee grounds or an open box of baking soda in the unused icebox keeps odor from developing. Make sure drain is clean and no leaks are present. Replace drain hose if required.
Refrigerator	Operation Cleanliness Lack of odor Frost build-up	Defrost if required. Clean and/or ventilate as described for icebox. Check connection to power source. If not operating check batteries with hydrometer; recharge if necessary. Replace blown fuses. If new fuse blows, correct short circuit and repair or replace defective wiring. If gas type, check pilot light and gas supply.
Sink, drains.	Cleanliness Operation Leaks Sea cocks operate normally	Clean with mild cleanser. Make sure drains are open and hoses do not leak. Replace defective hoses.
Galley and head pumps for fresh and salt water.	Operation Sea cock open on fresh water hose Odor from salt water pump	Pumps should operate smoothly and deliver water easily. Check fresh water tank for level of contents. Check water hoses for leaks; replace if required. Operate salt water pump daily to prevent odor.
Head	Operation Leaks Sea cocks operate normally	Be sure sea cocks are open before using head. Pumps should operate smoothly. Check for leaks in hoses and around gaskets. Replace hoses and gaskets if required. Replace defective valves. Do not leave sea cocks open between usages if head is below water line.
Log book	Current entries	The boat's log should contain daily entries of all pertinent information, even in port.

Basic Boat Maintenance - - J. Frank Brumbaugh

TABLE 2
WEEKLY PREVENTIVE MAINTENANCE

WEEKLY	INSPECT FOR	ACTION REQUIRED
Standing rigging	Loose, corroded, broken wires; loose chain plate bolts. Broken or dirty insulators in backstay radio antenna	Rigging should be unbroken and free of corrosion and correctly tensioned. Repair or replace damaged sections. Tighten bolts holding chain plates. Check connections between rigging and mast head; repair as required. Wipe salt from backstay insulators. Replace cracked or broken insulators.
Turnbuckles	Loose, broken, cotter pin or ring missing. Covering loose or torn	Tighten as required. Replace missing cotter pin or ring. Replace broken turnbuckle. Repair or replace covers.
Lifelines Stanchions Pulpits	Loose wires, bolts Bent stanchions Corrosion Missing hardware	Replace damaged parts. Tighten loose bolts and clamps. Replace missing hardware. Remove corrosion and oil metal lifelines slightly.
Running rigging	Chafed lines Broken or defective blocks	Replace chafed lines or turn end for end. Replace broken or defective parts. Lubricate cars, pulleys, blocks, capstans, winches, etc., as required.
Mooring, docking lines	Chafed Cut Damaged	Replace damaged lines. Retain old lines for spares or emergency use. Splice to length as required.
Signal haliards Flags Pennants	Damaged or missing	Repair or replace as required. Wash dirty flags and dry before stowing.
Shower Tubs Pumps Drains	Operation Leaks Open sea cocks	Shower and drain sump pumps should operate smoothly. Sea cocks must be open for some drains to function; close sea cocks when drains are not in use. Replace leaking hoses. Clean out stopped drain.

TABLE 2
WEEKLY PREVENTIVE MAINTENANCE

WEEKLY	INSPECT FOR	ACTION REQUIRED
Storage batteries	State of charge Corrosion Electrolyte level Mounting	Batteries must be solidly mounted so they cannot shift in heavy seas. Check specific gravity in each cell with Hydrometer and note reading in battery log. Use care not to spill electrolyte. Add distilled water to cells if needed. Check that all connections are tight. Brush off corrosion. Wipe tops of batteries with cloth dampened in solution of 2 teaspoons baking soda to one quart fresh water. Wipe exposed metal with silicone grease (Dow-Corning DC-3 or DC-4 or equivalent). If unavailable use petroleum jelly. Silicone grease lasts the life of the battery. Petroleum jelly melts off and must be replace periodically.
Electronic Equipment: Radio-telephone, direction finder, depth sounder, receivers, radar, loud hailer, LORAN, GPS, etc.	Proper operation Loose knobs Loose mountings Loose connections	All electronic equipment should be turned on for at least one hour each week to prevent damage from moisture. Operation can be checked while this is done. Refer to equipment instruction manuals for details of operation and maintenance. Tighten loose connections, mounting, knobs. Loose screws on the outside of the equipment should be tightened. *Do not adjust any screws inside the equipment* as damage may occur or complete realignment may be required. Many internal screws are adjustments which affect operation and should not be touched except by a trained technician.
Engines Battery charger Motorgenerator set Auxiliary engines	Smooth operation Oil and fuel levels Smoky exhaust RPM levels Synchronization	Engines should start easily and run smoothly. Exhaust should not smoke badly. Refer to engine instruction manuals or tune-up and overhaul instruction. See Tables 8 and 9 in this book for general troubleshooting of gasoline and diesel engines.

Basic Boat Maintenance - - J. Frank Brumbaugh

TABLE 3
MONTHLY PREVENTIVE MAINTENANCE

MONTHLY	INSPECT FOR	ACTION REQUIRED
Medical and first-aid supplies	Completeness Adequacy Freshness	Inventory medical supplies and drugs. Replace what has been used, is out of date, damaged, or rusty instruments. Make sure supplies and drugs are adequate for anticipated medical problems and accidents. Keep a sufficient supply of toiletries on hand.
Engine instruments Indicator lamps, etc.	Proper operation	Note operation of all engine instruments. Replace when necessary.
Hydraulic system	Operation Leaks Fluid level Correct pressure	Check fluid level and pressure. Check lines and fittings for leaks, weak or damaged sections. Replace as required.
Boarding ladder Swim ladder Gangplank	Condition	Repair noted damage. Surfaces of ladder, steps and gangplank should be non-skid.
Fuel supplies: Alcohol Kerosene Bottled gas Gasoline Motor oil	Quantity Secure stowage Leaks	Tanks must be securely mounted and vented. Tighten all connections and eliminate leaks. Replace defective lines, valves, fittings. clean filters. Spare cans of flammable liquids must be stowed so they cannot shift. Compartments must be ventilated to prevent accumulation of an explosive atmosphere.
Ground tackle Anchors Chains Rodes Shackles Swivels, etc.	Damage Corrosion Chafing Missing parts Stowage	Anchors must be stowed where they can be reached for immediate use. Standard anchor and lunch hook may be carried in chocks on deck or lashed to pulpit or rigging. Anchors and chain must be kept free of rust and not stowed near the compass. Shackles secured with cotter pins or rings or copper wire should be checked. Check swivel between anchor and all-chain rode (never use a swivel between the anchor and a twisted nylon rode for hockles can occur which greatly weaken the rode). Worn fiber lines can be turned end for end after one season's use. Chafed portions of fiber rodes should be cut away and a thimble spliced in the remaining end. Bitter ends of all anchor rodes must be bent to the mast, mooring bitts, Sampson post, or an eye bolt in the frame of the boat before casting the anchor over the side.

TABLE 3
MONTHLY PREVENTIVE MAINTENANCE

MONTHLY	INSPECT FOR	ACTION REQUIRED
Cleats Bitts Chocks All deck hardware	Loose, missing hardware Broken	Tighten loose hardware. Remove cleats and bed in compound if leaks develop where they are mounted. Smooth insides of chocks to prevent line chafing. Use hardwood backing blocks inside hull when mounted deck hardware on fiberglass or plywood decks.
Skylights Windows Port lights All glass and plastic	Cleanliness Broken glass Defective seals Scratched Discolored Hardware loose or missing	Clean glass and plastic with fresh water to remove salt. Use care when cleaning plastic to prevent scratching. Replace defective seals and leaky bedding, broken glass or broken or scratched plastic.
Fenders Fender boards	Damaged Missing grommets	Visually inspect fenders, and fender boards. Repair or replace as required.
Sea anchor	Tears Holes Broken frame Mold Mildew Missing parts Corrosion	Inspect sea anchor. Repair or replace as required.
Life preservers and rings Buoyant cushions	General condition Punctures Water logging Tears, rips Missing straps or hardware Mildew	Replace defective items. Repair minor damage. All life saving items must bear U.S. Coast Guard Approval.
Spars	Loose or missing hardware Breaks Dents Corrosion Bends Loose sail tracks	Replace or tighten hardware. Remove corrosion from metal spars and paint with anticorrosive primer or paint. Have breaks repaired or replace spar. Straighten and tighten sail tracks.
Topsides, decks, rails	Slippery spots Open seams Flaking paint Loose hardware	Caulk seams if required. Apply non-skid material in slippery spots. Paint as required. Tighten or rebed and replace loose hardware. Wax fiberglass if needed.
Waterline Boot topping	Marine growths Oil residue	Use nylon or fiber bristle brush to scrub down the waterline to remove marine growths and scum. Efforts should extend one or two feet below waterline. If done more often than monthly this will greatly extend periods between bottom painting. Removal of growth lightens the boat, saves fuel, and increases speed through water.

TABLE 3
MONTHLY PREVENTIVE MAINTENANCE

MONTHLY	INSPECT FOR	ACTION REQUIRED
Medical and first-aid supplies	Completeness Adequacy Freshness	Inventory medical supplies and drugs. Replace what has been used, is out of date, damaged, or rusty instruments. Make sure supplies and drugs are adequate for anticipated medical problems and accidents. Keep a sufficient supply of toiletries on hand.
Engine instruments Indicator lamps, etc.	Proper operation	Note operation of all engine instruments. Replace when necessary.
Hydraulic system	Operation Leaks Fluid level Correct pressure	Check fluid level and pressure. Check lines and fittings for leaks, weak or damaged sections. Replace as required.
Boarding ladder Swim ladder Gangplank	Condition	Repair noted damage. Surfaces of ladder, steps and gangplank should be non-skid.
Fuel supplies: Alcohol Kerosene Bottled gas Gasoline Motor oil	Quantity Secure stowage Leaks	Tanks must be securely mounted and vented. Tighten all connections and eliminate leaks. Replace defective lines, valves, fittings, clean filters. Spare cans of flammable liquids must be stowed so they cannot shift. Compartments must be ventilated to prevent accumulation of an explosive atmosphere.
Ground tackle Anchors Chains Rodes Shackles Swivels, etc.	Damage Corrosion Chafing Missing parts Stowage	Anchors must be stowed where they can be reached for immediate use. Standard anchor and lunch hook may be carried in chocks on deck or lashed to pulpit or rigging. Anchors and chain must be kept free of rust and not stowed near the compass. Shackles secured with cotter pins or rings or copper wire should be checked. Check swivel between anchor and all-chain rode (never use a swivel between the anchor and a twisted nylon rode for hockles can occur which greatly weaken the rode). Worn fiber lines can be turned end for end after one season's use. Chafed portions of fiber rodes should be cut away and a thimble spliced in the remaining end. Bitter ends of all anchor rodes must be bent to the mast, mooring bitts, Sampson post, or an eye bolt in the frame of the boat before casting the anchor over the side.

TABLE 3
MONTHLY PREVENTIVE MAINTENANCE

MONTHLY	INSPECT FOR	ACTION REQUIRED
Berths, mattresses, leeboards, pillows	Mildew Rips Tears or holes Open seams	Treat as required with anti-mildew liquid or spray. Repair or replace as required.
Carpets Rugs Curtains, curtain rods	Dirt Stains Burns Holes Rips Missing hardware Corrosion on metal parts	Launder if dirty. Remove stains. Repair or replace as required. Remove corrosion from rods. Replace missing hardware.
Bedding Towels, etc.	Mildew Tears, holes	Air in sunlight to freshen. Stow only in well ventilated lockers or bins. Repair minor defects. Replace mildewed or worn-out items.
Lockers Drawers	Ventilation Easy access Loose or missing hardware	Make certain contents do not block ventilation holes. Lubricate slides and hinges if required. Tighten or replace damaged hardware. Use *Lysol* deodorant spray or equivalent to eliminate musty odors. Discard unwanted contents; do not let lockers, drawers and bins accumulate unnecessary junk!
Fans	Operation Dust	Clean blades, guards, and bodies to remove oily dirt. Lubricate if required. Fans should operation quietly and smoothly. If fuses blow and wiring is not defective, fan must be repaired or replaced.
Staple foods Canned goods	Spoilage Rust Swollen or dented cans Insects in dry foods	Inspect all dry and canned foods. Discard swollen, badly dented, or rusty cans, and dried foods containing insects. Inventory supplies and purchase replacements to bring quanities up to normal. Spray stowage area to eliminate insects. (Do not spray insecticide on food or dishes.)
Tobacco, matches, cigarettes, liquor	Mold Dampness Quantity on hand	Discard damaged goods and purchase replacements to bring inventory to normal.
Signal flares Distress rockets Smoke grenades Signal flags Dye markers Shark repellent	Condition Quantity Age Dampness	Discard and replace damp, damaged, and overage pyrotechnics and dye markers. Repair or replace damaged or missing signal flags.

Basic Boat Maintenance - - *J. Frank Brumbaugh*

TABLE 3 MONTHLY PREVENTIVE MAINTENANCE		
MONTHLY	**INSPECT FOR**	**ACTION REQUIRED**
Firearms Ammunition Flare launcher	Rust Corrosion Broken or missing parts Dented ammunition	Discard and replace dented or badly corroded ammunition. Clean and oil firearms and flare launcher. Replace all broken or missing parts. NOTE: Arms and ammunition should be kept in a lockable locker, well ventilated.
Fishing tackle	Broken, missing parts Corrosion Quantities of hooks, lures, lines, leaders, sinkers, etc.	Clean and lubricate reels. Clean rods. Repair loose guides and bindings. Remove corrosion from reel seat. Check tackle for condition and quantities and replace or add to as required.
Flashlights All dry cell batteries Spare bulbs	Operation Age and condition of batteries	Check operation of flashlights. Replace bulbs and batteries as required. Replace unused dry cell batteries one year or more old. Use if possible but old batteries are undependable in emergencies.
Tools	Rust Corrosion Condition	Remove rust and corrosion and lightly oil all tools. Lubricate moving parts of adjustable tools. sharpen all edged tools. Clean files and rasps and oil lightly.
Cooking utensils, dishes Cutlery	Broken Missing Rust or corrosion Sharpness of knives	Scour to remove rust and corrosion. Replace cracked, broken, or missing items. Sharpen knives. Apply a light coating of vegetable oil or shortening to blades of carbon steel (not necessary with stainless steel knives).
Clocks Watches Barometer All weather instruments	Operation Condition	Check operation and condition. Repair or replace defective items. Set operating clocks and watches to local time and adjust if required. Compare barometer reading with official Coast Guard or Weather Service barometer reading and correct if required.
Piloting instruments Dividers Rulers Plotters Slide rules Pencils Erasers Pencil sharpeners Binoculars, etc.	Condition Quantity	Check condition and quantity. Replace as required.

Basic Boat Maintenance - - J. Frank Brumbaugh

TABLE 4
ANNUAL OR START OF CRUISE PREVENTIVE MAINTENANCE

YEARLY OR START OF CRUISE	INSPECT FOR	ACTION REQUIRED
Overall checkout	See next column	Perform all preventive maintenance procedures given in Tables 1, 2, and 3. Then proceed with remainder in this table. These procedures should be performed before each cruise which takes the boat out of sight of land and which is expected to last one or more weeks.
Hull Bottom paint Depth sounder transducer	Soundness of hull and paint condition Amount of marine growth on bottom	Renew bottom paint as required, usually at six months to two-year intervals, depending on conditions in cruising waters. Boat must be careened or hauled out for bottom to be scraped and painted. Caulk seams before painting wooden hull. Follow directions of paint manufacturer and use good quality paint. CAUTION: do not paint surface of depth sounder transducer.
Protective zincs	Condition	If badly pitted and corroded, replace zincs on rudder, shaft, strut, keel, etc.
Wiring Junction boxes	Condition Tight connections	Inspect all wiring throughout the boat and all connections, including within junction boxes. Wiring should be free of chafe and bare spots exept where connections are made. Long runs of wiring must be supported at 14-inch (maximum) intervals by nonmetallic clips or clamps. No wires should enter the bilges except those to bilge pumps and water alarms.
Charts, books, navigational publications	Condition Completeness Type Current issues	Charts must be on board for all waters expected to be sailed, and corrected to include latest changes in *Notices to Mariners*. Pilot books and Sailing Directions must cover cruising waters and be latest edition or corrected to date of sailing. All books and publications used in navigation must be current issues. This is particularly important for the *Nautical Almanac* and *Tide Tables*.
Spares Lines, hardware, spare parts, etc.	Condition Quantity Completeness	Inventory all spares and make certain sufficient of each are on board. Spare bulbs, fuses, dry cell batteries, lines, chain, cotter pins and rings, shackles, swivels, hooks, snaps, rings, cleats, bitts, blocks, pulleys, screws, nuts, bolts, washers, bedding compound, gaskets, engine spares, head spares, stove spares, rigging wire and clamps, thimbles, marline, oakum, caulking cotton, paints, glue, tape, canvas, shock cord and hooks, fiberglass cloth, mat and tape, sail repair materials, electrical spares, pump spares, generator and alternator brushes, paint brushes, etc., must be checked and proper amounts of each applicable item stowed on board.

TABLE 4
ANNUAL OR START OF CRUISE PREVENTIVE MAINTENANCE

YEARLY OR START OF CRUISE	INSPECT FOR	ACTION REQUIRED
Stores Fresh water	Quantity Condition Stowage	Inventory all stores of food and fresh water, liquor, fuel, oil, matches, paper products, and other expendable items. All must be in good condition and quantities sufficient for twice the time estimated at sea before making the next landfall. Fresh water should be calculated at a minimum of one-half gallon per person per day for twice the estimated number of days at sea. Fuel and oil requirements depend upon past usage. Two gallons of alcohol are sufficient to prime a two-burner kerosene galley stove three times a day for a year. Kerosene is widely available, but alcohol is difficult to locate outside U.S. waters. Dry foods must be stowed in waterproof containers. Cans should be marked with contents and paper lables removed. Contents of glass jars and bottles should be repackaged in plastic containers if possible. Fresh eggs should be wiped with mineral oil or dropped into boiling water for five seconds before stowing them in a cool, dark place. Slab bacon and chunk cheese wrapped in cheesecloth wrung out in vinegar will be resistant to mold. Potatoes and citrus should be stowed in the dark. Store onions in a mesh bag in good ventilation under normal lighting. Fresh foods requiring refrigeration must be used before ice is gone and they begin to spoil.
Main engine(s)	Condition Operation	Main engines should be tuned up and adjusted for proper operation. Plugs and points, or fuel injectors, must be new or clean and adjusted properly. All bolts must be tight and gaskets in good condition. Oil and oil filters should be changed if required. Replace thermostat each year. Clean fuel filters. Check fuel lines and fittings for leaks. Check exhaust lines and connections for leaks and for proper water flow in water-cooled exhausts. Clean drip pan beneath engines. Check backfire screen on carburetor. Adjust throttle linkage. Replace worn veebelts. Check transmission grease level and smoothness of operation. Be sure to use the proper fuel-to-oil mixture for 2-cycle engines, and the proper weight motor oil in the crankcase of 4-cycle gasoline engines. Gasoline purchased in foreign ports should be strained through chamois to remove water and foreign materials before putting in your tanks. Lighter weights of diesel oil are not always available in foreign ports but kerosene can be used instead of No. 1 or No. 2 diesel oil, and kerosene is available practically everywhere in the world. NOTE: Always follow engine manufacturer's instructions for tune-up, overhaul, oil change, operating speed, etc.

TABLE 4
ANNUAL OR START OF CRUISE PREVENTIVE MAINTENANCE

YEARLY OR START OF CRUISE	INSPECT FOR	ACTION REQUIRED
Small gasoline engines used to charge batteries, drive electrical generators, winches, outboards, etc.	Condition Operation Cleanliness Brushes Connections	All small gasoline engines should be tuned up and have new plugs installed. Magnetoes and points must be in good condition. Two-cycle engines require that fuel be mixed at a definite ratio with the proper weight oil. Oil changes and other periodic maintenance depend upon hours of use and the engine manufacturer's recommendations should be followed if available; otherwise, refer to Chapter IX for information. Strain foreign-purchased gasoline through chamois to remove water and foreign materials before using.
Generators Alternators Dynamotors All electric motors	Condition Operation Cleanliness Brushes Connections	Generators and alternators, whether driven by main or auxiliary engines, must be checked for proper operation. Brushes must be of sufficient length. There should be no sparking at the commutator or slip rings. Mica spacers must be below the level of commutator, or must be undercut. Commutator should be smooth and chocolate brown in color. Assembly and mounting bolts must be tight. Drive belts should be in good condition and have proper tension. Housing and surroundings must be kept clean and dry. Lubricate as recommended by the manufacturer. Do not over lubricate.
Licenses Registrations Permits, passports Innoculation records, etc.	Renewal dates	Note renewal and expirations dates on boat's calendar sufficiently in advance to allow time for processing. Make certain all necessary papers are aboard before going foreign.
Propellers and shafts	Nicks Dents, corrosion Operation Lubrication Shear pins	Shafts should be smooth and run true. Shaft log packing should be checked and repacked if necessary. Remove corrosion. Smooth out nicks in propeller blades and reshape, repair, or replace as required. Carry a spare propeller on long cruises.
Dinghy Tender Life rafts Floats	Condition Stowage Lashings Lines Hardware Supplies	Inspect for damage and completeness of life support supplies. Tighten or replace hardware. Paint as required. Bottom paint should be applied to dinghy or tender when boat is hauled or carreened for painting. Replace damaged lines. Make certain lashings hold securely but are easy to unship in an emergency.
Emergency food, water signals, etc.	Completeness Adequacy Age or damage	Inventory emergency life-support stores and equipment. Be sure water, food, distress signals, and lantern or flashlight batteries are fresh. Stow where they can be together and can be easily grabbed in an emergency but where they will not be used casually.
Air conditioner	Refrigerant level Lubrication Brushes or compressor Motor Leaks Cooling Worn belts Clean filter	Add refrigerant to proper level if needed. Motor brushes must be of sufficient length or replaced. Replace worn belts. Check tubing and connections and replace if leaky. Tighten connections as needed. Clean or replace filters.

DATE	CELL #	BATTERY # 1	BATTERY # 2	BATTERY # 3	BATTERY # 4
JAN 22 2000	1	12.00	12.05	12.05	12.00
	2	12.05	12.05	12.00	12.00
	3	12.10	12.10	12.05	12.05
	4	12.00	12.05	12.00	12.00
	5	12.10	12.00	12.00	12.00
	6	12.05	12.05	12.05	12.00

Figure 1

Weekly battery log.

DATE	FUEL	ENGINE HOURS START	ENGINE HOURS STOP	TACH	HOURS RUN	TOTAL ENGINE HOURS
1-22	X	116.8	121.2	3800	4.6	273.5
1-23	21.9	121.2	125	2200	3.8	277.3

Figure 2

Engine hour log.

CHAPTER TWO
HULL AND TOPSIDE

The hull and topside of a modern boat are seldom the source of trouble. Fiberglass boats rarely have deck leaks and are difficult to hole. If water cannot gain entrance through hatches and ventilators there will seldom be water in the bilges except the small amount trickling through the shaft log which serves to lubricate the propeller shaft. Steel and aluminum boats have equally tight hulls. Boats with wooden hulls may be expected to have minor leaks resulting from the normal working of the planks. Occasional pumping of the bilges will be necessary and this can easily be accomplished by an automatic bilge pump.

Wooden hulls are subject to dry rot which is caused by a fungus active in the presence of fresh water, warmth, darkness, and lack of ventilation. Rock salt strewn in the bilge water of a wooden boat used in fresh water will aid in preventing rot since the fungus cannot grow in salt water. Wooden boats kept in salt water will not benefit from the addition of rock salt.

Dry rot makes the wood soft and pithy, leaves it without strength, and has a peculiar, musty odor. Rotten wood must be removed when it is found. There are several liquid products on the market which can be applied to dry rot to kill the fungus and harden and strengthen the rotted wood. Choose a product recommended by a marine dealer for this purpose.

Extensive dry rot, especially in planks, stringers, ribs, or keelson require the rotted portion be removed and replaced by sound timbers. This is usually not within the capability of most boat owners and should be done by a qualified yard.

Dry rot is expensive to cure and can be dangerous since it weakens the boat so she may be stove in a blow. Dry rot can be prevented by ensuring excellent ventilation throughout the boat, protecting wood surfaces with paint or varnish, and eliminating areas of contact between wood and fresh water. The interiors of wooden boats covered with fiberglass are as susceptible to dry rot as other wooden boats.

Wood fittings are more extensive in steel and aluminum than in fiberglass boats. Painting, varnishing, and good ventilation will protect this wood from the effects of dry rot. The hulls of wooden boats with lapstrake or carvel planking must be kept properly caulked. Strip-built and molded plywood hulls remain watertight without caulking. Caulking cotton set in wet paint is usually used in the seams of small boats. Oakum set in pitch is used on larger hulls. While caulking is not too difficult to learn, it is a lengthy job and must be correctly done. Too little caulking will allow a seam to leak. Too much will be squeezed out of the seam by swelling planks and cause a leak. For most owners of wooden hulls, caulking can best be done by a qualified yard.

Repairs to the hulls of steel and aluminum boats must be made by welding or riveting. These repairs should also be made by a qualified yard.

Fiberglass is used for the hulls and decks of the majority of small boats afloat today. Actually, the hull material is plastic which is reinforced by fiberglass mat, cloth, and roving, much as concrete is reinforced by steel rods and mesh. Fiberglass reinforced plastic has a great many advantages when used for boat hulls, decks, and superstructure:

It is leak proof and water tight.

It is impervious to attack by marine worms and borers.

It is very lightweight compared to equal-strength structures in wood or metal.

It is flexible and resists damage from blows which affect large surfaces, and which could hole a hull of other material.

Color can be molded into the material.

It is translucent in light colors and allows much more light to penetrate below decks.

It is easily molded in compound curves which aid in turning the force of the seas.

It is molded with a smooth, glassy surface which allows greater speeds by reducing water friction and makes adherence of marine growths more difficult.

It is rot proof and waterproof, because it does not soak up water like wood.

It is easily repaired by the average boat owner.

It can be used to form tanks and furnishings when the boat is built, with these molded in place.

It requires only a bottom paint to prevent the growth of marine animals and vegetation.

It is resistant to many mild acids, alkalis, and cleaning and waxing are easy.

All underwater portions of boat hulls, regardless of the materials from which they are constructed, require painting with good quality bottom paint to retard marine growth. All hull materials require one coat or more of primer before the bottom paint is applied. Primers are used to ensure adhesion of the bottom paint and to prevent galvanic corrosion on metal hulls. A suitable primer is usually used on steel hulls. Zinc chromate is used as a primer on aluminum hulls. Special primers for wood and fiberglass are available and should be used on these materials. The recommendation of the paint manufacturer should be followed carefully as to the primer used, the method of application of primer and bottom paint, the number of coats of each, and whether the boat should be launched while the bottom paint is wet, tacky, or has dried thoroughly.

Bottom paint may contain metallic copper or chemicals which retard marine growth. It is available in many colors and types. Price is a reasonably reliable guide to quality. A top quality bottom paint may cost $200 or more per gallon. The brand and quality of the bottom paint you buy depends primarily upon the waters in which you normally cruise. Additional factors which will affect your choice are whether you trail your boat to and from the water; whether the water is fresh, brackish, or salt; and whether the waters are temperate or tropical. Recommendations by skippers of commercial boats in your cruising waters are generally valid. Boat yards' and other boat owners' recommendations may be prejudiced but a consensus will indicate the best type and grade, if not brand, for your boat.

Almost any inexpensive bottom paint will suffice if you trail your boat to and from fresh water, and a slightly better grade will be adequate if you trail to and from salt water. The highest quality paint you can afford should be used if your boat remains in tropical or semitropical salt water all the time. Somewhat lower quality will suffice in colder waters. An intermediate quality paint will be adequate even in southern waters if you move between fresh and salt water and remain in each for several days. Marine growths which attach themselves in salt water will die when exposed to fresh water, and vice versa.

Read the brochures distributed by various paint manufacturers. This knowledge, along with familiarity with your own cruising waters and conversations with other boat owners, will enable you to make a responsible choice of the type, grade, and brand of bottom paint best for your boat in those waters.

The hull must be prepared before painting if satisfactory results are to be achieved. Marine growth must be removed while still wet and as soon as possible after the hull is clear of the water. It will be much easier to scrape off before it dries. Nothing sticks tighter than the base of a barnacle which has been allowed to dry for a day or two. Use a dull scraper which will not gouge or damage the hull. Work as quickly as possible, keeping the bottom wet with a hose if it starts to dry. Scrape until the hull feels relatively smooth to your bare hand. Then wash the bottom well with detergent and water, using a stiff bristled brush. Rinse well and allow to dry thoroughly before applying primer or bottom paint.

Remaining old paint may be scraped or sanded from wood and fiberglass hulls, or a paint remover used which will not damage or soften the plastic resins in a fiberglass hull. Paint may be burned from a wooden hull if extreme care is taken to prevent fire. A plumber's burner can be rented inexpensively and is faster and much easier to use than the usual blow torch.

Steel and aluminum hulls should be sand blasted to remove old paint. Metal must be clean and dry and free of oil before primer is applied.

Follow the paint manufacturer's recommendations when preparing and painting the hull. Coverage to be expected for bottom paint may be calculated simply by multiplying the waterline length by the draft, and then multiplying by 3.5. Divide the answer you get by the coverage in square feet per gallon stated by the manufacturer. This final answer is the number of gallons of paint required for one coat.

The amount of paint required for one coat topsides can be calculated by multiplying the length overall by the beam, then multiply this product by 1.5. Divide this answer by the coverage in square feet per gallon stated by the manufacturer. The final answer is the number of gallons of topsides paint needed for a single coat.

Fiberglass topsides seldom require painting and are usually waxed instead. A paste wax is best. The job is similar in all respects to waxing an automobile. Marine waxes containing carnauba wax are longest lasting. Wax should also be used below decks on bulkheads, overheads, lockers, etc. Any wood trim on a fiberglass boat will be easier to finish properly if it can be removed.

Teak trim requires no finishing. Teak decks need only washing occasionally, and care taken that nothing oily is dripped on the deck. Commercial teak cleaners may be used rarely and sparingly. A teak hull does require bottom paint to retard marine growth but teak is somewhat immune to teredoes, other worms and borers. No other protection is necessary for teak.

Topsides and decks should be washed down with fresh water weekly and when returning from a sail, if possible. This rinsing is all that is usually required for fiberglass boats. Topsides and decks of other than fiberglass require scrubbing once a week, and touching up with paint as required.

Glass and plastic windows, skylights, portlights, etc., should be rinsed with fresh water to remove salt encrustations. Household window cleaners, without ammonia, are also useful. Care must be taken that soft plastic windows are not scratched.

Nonskid areas of decks must be maintained for safety. Adhesive-backed nonskid material is available and may be self-adhered in desired positions on smooth decks. These are usually used on fiberglass decks. Abrasive particles added to deck paint are commercially available and may be used on all deck materials. Some commercial boats mix clean sand, sawdust, or crushed nut shells into deck paint to achieve a safe, non-slippery surface, but this is less attractive than using the abrasive additives available from marine paint dealers.

Deck hardware such as cleats, fairleads, etc., should be solidly mounted in a sealant or bedding compound to eliminate leaks around mounting hardware. If not mounted directly to a structural portion of the boat, and especially in fiberglass decks, all deck hardware subject to any strain must be through-bolted with a backup block of hardwood or aluminum. Use large flat washers and split lock washers or a locking nut on each fastener.

A teak grating, provides secure, comfortable footing in a self-bailing cockpit. Wood other than teak must be painted and should have a nonskid surface.

Decks must be kept clear of odds and ends at all times so one may walk about safely. Lines should be coiled or faked down if they must be handy on deck, but otherwise should be stowed out of the way where they can be found when needed. Lines should not be Flemished down when at sea although this is often done with inboard ends of mooring lines when docked. Flemished lines should be moved daily to prevent discoloration of the deck or the formation of mildew.

Anchors should be lashed in chocks, or may be lashed to the pulpit or shrouds. The boathook and swab, or its handle, should be lashed in the shrouds where they will be easy to access but out of the way. A life ring or horseshoe float should be secured near the helmsman with easily broken lashings so it can be tossed readily to anyone going over the side. A 60- to 100-foot length of polyethylene floating line, should be attached to the life ring and coiled so it will payout freely when the life ring goes by the board. The stern pulpit or shrouds of a sailboat, or the cockpit or cabin side of a power boat, will provide good locations for life rings.

The dinghy is a major problem for smaller boats. It may best be stowed and lashed upside down on the cabin top or foredeck. Towing the dinghy is an art which few have mastered, and is not recommended except in calm waters. An inflatable boat or life raft folds into a compact bundle when deflated and is a serviceable tender for boats not able to carry a rigid dinghy in davits or cradle on board. All rigid dinghies require bottom paint, and the paint will last a lot longer if the dinghy is not kept in the water all the time, usually about twice as long as the paint on the hull of the larger boat. The dinghy gunwale should be edged with large diameter cotton rope, fiber or rubber hose, to prevent damage to topsides when the dinghy is tied along side. The dinghy must be kept clean inside and out and its painter in good condition. Old anchor rodes or mooring lines can also be used as painters but are usually of much larger diameter than required for tying up the dinghy.

Gangplanks and boarding or swimming ladders also present a stowage problem best met by the ingenuity of each boat owner. The surface of the gangplank and steps of ladders must be kept skid-proof. Paint mixed with abrasive powder or self-adhesive nonskid strips are ideal for both. Small cleats of half or three-quarter-inch square wood should be attached across of the gangplank at 14- to 18-inch intervals.

A narrow but sturdy gangplank can double as a fender board, thus saving stowage space and cost. Half-circular cutouts staggered along the edges of the gangplank will not greatly weaken it if made of one-inch thick marine plywood and this allows it to be used as a boarding or swimming ladder, further reducing cost and stowage problems. A section of one-inch marine (not exterior grade) plywood eight feet long and eighteen inches wide is suggested as a combination gangplank/fender board/boarding ladder. Rig eyebolts or holes in all four corners allow it to be lashed in place as ladder or gangplank, and for hanging from deck cleats when used as a fender board.

Keep a sturdy bucket handy for bringing sea water aboard for sloshing down decks, washing fish blood out of the cockpit, washing clothes and dishes, bathing on deck, etc. A lanyard of 3/8-inch line spliced to thimbles and having a snap hook at each end should be secured to the bail of the bucket and to the lifeline or a ring bolt in the cockpit. This prevents loss of the bucket and makes taking seawater aboard much easier. Plastic buckets, or steel buckets which have been hot dip galvanized are both excellent, although the plastic bucket's bail is not so strongly attached, and the galvanized bucket will eventually rust. Folding canvas buckets have neither of these disadvantages but are somewhat difficult to submerge when tossed over the side. Keep the bucket clean and dry and the lanyard attached at both ends all the time on deck.

The tiller must be kept varnished or painted to prevent deterioration and splitting. A spare tiller should always be carried in case of breakage or loss overboard. Boats having wheel steering, whether hydraulic, geared, chain and sprocket, or cable and drum, require periodic inspection of the steering mechanism for damage. Gears, pulleys, and bearings must be kept lubricated at all times to prevent wear and make for smooth steering. Rudder pintle hardware must be kept tight and replaced when corroded or broken. The rudder should be scraped and painted when the bottom is painted. Do not paint over protective zincs on metal rudders.

Propeller blades should be inspected for nicks

and bending and corrosion removed when the boat is hauled. Nuts should be tight, shear pins in place and bearings in good condition. The shaft should run true and smoothly. Zincs should be attached to shaft and strut for protection against galvanic corrosion.

The copper radio ground plate or pipe should be scraped free of marine growth and sanded clean when the boat is hauled. Never apply paint to ground plates nor to the surface of depth sounder transducers.

Outboard engines should be tilted free of the water when not in use. Corrosion and marine growth should be scraped from underwater parts whenever an accumulation is noted. The outboard should be covered or removed from its mounting bracket and stowed out of the weather when on an extended voyage under sail. The outboard on a sailboat is seldom used except when maneuvering in a harbor. Do not stow the outboard closer than six feet to the boat's compass since it may cause the compass to give incorrect indications.

CHAPTER THREE
SAILS, RIGGING, AND GROUND TACKLE

Modern sails are made of synthetic fibers, usually either Dacron or nylon. Synthetic sails are strong, light, and will not mildew. They can be furled or bagged while wet without rot or loss of strength, although they should be dried first, if possible. Sunlight is the major enemy of modern sailcloth and exposure to sunlight gradually weakens the fibers. Weakened seams can split and weakened sails may blow out in heavy weather. For these reasons sails should always be covered when not in use. Sails furled on a rod stay and not covered will gradually be attacked by sunlight and weakened. The ultraviolet content of sunlight attacks synthetic sails, the same content which produces the deep tanning of the skin and is a major cause of skin aging and melanoma.

Sails should be made by a sail maker. It is not a job for an amateur. Sails must be designed for the specific boat and for certain conditions of sailing. This latter requirement has resulted in a proliferation of different sail types and cloth weights for the typical sailboat: Working jib, storm jib, genoa, spinnaker, working mainsail, storm trysail, staysails, etc., are used on the simplest rigged sail boats -- the Marconi-rigged, single masted sloop. The catboat uses a single sail rigged to a single mast stepped well forward, but since it is not usually used for cruising or racing, this type rig is not considered here, although it is simpler than the sloop rig. Ketches and yawls add mizzen and mizzen staysails to the foregoing list, and these boats have a second, shorter mast stepped abaft the mainmast. The mizzen mast is stepped forward of the rudder post in a ketch, and abaft the rudder post in a yawl.

The sails used most often are called *working sails* and consist of jib, main, and mizzen if two masts are stepped. This single set of sails is sufficient for most wind conditions while cruising. However, a suit of storm sails and an extra working jib will result in a well-found cruising boat. The jib and main can be winged out on opposite sides of the boat while running before the wind, or twin jibs flown wing-and-wing with the mainsail furled on the boom and covered.

Spinnakers and genoa jibs are used for running and the genoa can also be used on a reach. These are light air sails and are relatively fragile -- especially balloon spinnakers -- and very costly. They are used mainly for racing, although the large genoa rigged to a furling rod forestay can take the place of several different jibs, depending on the area of sail exposed to the wind.

Sails should be inspected visually every time they are hauled up or furled. Seams with loose threads should be resewn when first noted. When sewing synthetic fabric be sure to use the same thread material from which the cloth is woven; i.e., Dacron thread for Dacron sails, nylon thread for nylon cloth, etc. Pay particular attention to seams holding the boltrope, the headboard, and at tack and clew. Batten pockets should be inspected for ripping. Battens must have smooth surfaces and be inserted fully into the proper pockets. Battens should be removed before furling or bagging a sail. Reef points should be closely observed for broken threads and the reef lines replaced as necessary. Reef points are not included on sails made for boats with roller reefing.

The strength inherent in the fibers from which synthetic sails are made retard ripping when a small tear occurs, but all tears and rips must be repaired when first noted or they will become enlarged, further weaken the sail.

The following items are required for sail repair and are sold separately as well as in kits by many marine supply stores: Palm, beeswax, straight and curved needles, thread of various fibers, knife, and synthetic tape and cloth. Wide adhesive tape or duct tape is often used to effect temporary repairs during races. Most often sail repairs needed are confined to resewing rips, and replacing and sewing grommets. Large holes are rare and most often result from burning or melting when the sailcloth comes into contact with an open flame, a hot soldering iron or torch, etc. Sailcloth strips or tape are used as backing when repairing a rip or tear to reinforce the damaged portion of the sail.

There are several simple stitches you should be familiar with which are used in repairing sails, stitching canvas, making awnings, dodgers, ice and sail bags, etc.

The locking stitch, illustrated in Figure 3, is most often used in restitching seams and making bags. It is strong and the seam will not loosen if the thread breaks.

The running stitch, Figure 4, is used where extra strength or the locking feature of Figure 3 is not required, such as hemming edges of awnings, bags, etc. It may be used to secure the edges of a patch covering a rip although the round stitch of Figure 5 is preferred for this purpose.

The herringbone stitch, Figure 6, is preferred for closing a tear and sewing the edge of a tear to the cloth reinforcement. Note adjacent stitches are staggered to avoid weakening the cloth near the tear. The cloth patch shown should be sewn to the sail using the round stitch of Figure 5.

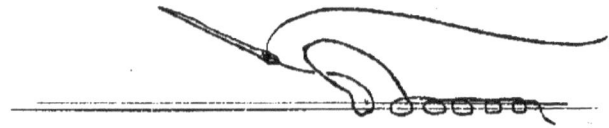

Figure 3. Locking Stitch

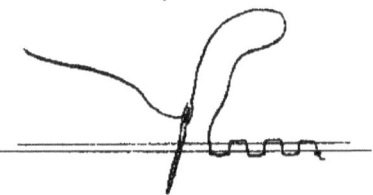

Figure 4. Running Stitch.

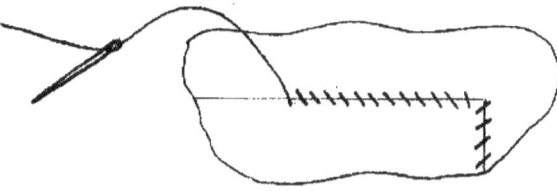

Figure 5. Round Stitch

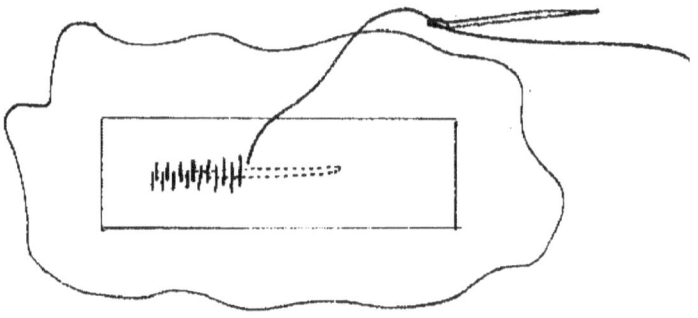

Figure 6. Herringbone Stitch

Figures 3 through 6

Figure 7 illustrates the steps required in repairing

a tear in a sail. Fold under a narrow edge of each side of the tear and crease the folds with the side of a knife blade so they will remain folded (A). Place the patch beneath the tear (B). Pull the folded edges of the tear together and sew tear and patch together with the herringbone stitch (C). Turn the sail over with the patch on top and sew the edge of the patch to the sail with a round stitch (D).

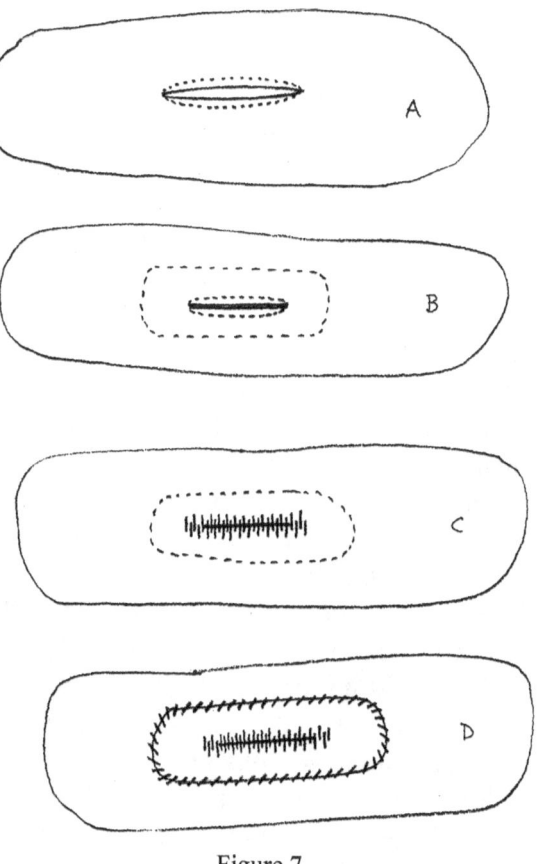

Figure 7

Repairing a Ripped Sail.
Three-cornered or L-shaped tears are repaired the same as the simple, straight tear illustrated in Figure 7.

Holes in sails where material is missing may be patched similarly to simple tears. Fold material around the hole under and crease with knife blade. Sew the edge of the hole to the patch with a round stitch. Sew the edges of the patch to the sail, also using the round stitch.

Temporary repairs for a ripped sail can be made using cloth adhesive tape such as duct tape, Borden's *Mystic Tape,* Permacel Brand *Silvercel* tape, or equivalent, using tape about two inches wide. Prepare the tear as shown in Figure 7 (B) and apply the tape firmly to both sides. The sail should be completely dry for best results. This repair is a temporary measure and the tear should be repaired properly as soon as possible.

The running end of the thread remaining after sewing must be secured so it will not unravel. Several lock stitches taken in the same spot will hold after the thread is cut. Another method, borrowed from ladies' embroidery stitches is the French Knot. Run the needle up part way through the cloth near where the standing part of the thread emerges, and on the same side. Drop three half-hitches of the standing part of the thread over the point of the needle, snugging up each hitch as it is made. Pull the needle and thread up through the hitches just made, holding the three hitches against the cloth, and cut off the thread above the hitches. This effectively knots what was the running end of the thread.

Sails should not only be protected by covers and bags when not in use, but care should be taken not to carry more sail than conditions of wind and sea warrant. Since each boat is different from every other, even sister ships, and different skippers have different amounts of experience, no specific rules can be given which would always be applicable. Racing boats often carry sails longer in heavier weather than is prudent, taking calculated risks seemingly unwarranted by their chances of winning a race. Skippers of cruising boats are more prudent. Perhaps the best general rule is this: If you wonder whether it is time to shorten sail, it is; and if you wonder whether you should douse sails and heave to, you should. You will seldom be wrong in following this rule, and almost never place your boat in an avoidable dangerous situation.

Sail covers and sail bags should be made of the same material as sails, and must be kept in repair. Sails not in use should be bagged and stowed below decks or in a sail locker. Sails should be packed in bags so the head and clew are at the mouth of the bag and boltropes or slides can be fixed to the mast and boom without spilling the sail completely out of the bag.

Awnings, cockpit and rail dodgers, wind sails, curtains, convertible top, and all other "canvas" goods should be made of synthetic fiber cloth. All must be kept in good repair. Most repairs will be resewing seams and repairing rips, and occasional replacement of a grommet. Shoe bags, ice bags, and sea bags should be made of nylon, but heavy duty cotton canvas, treated to prevent mildew, serves nearly as well.

Brass grommets are made in two pieces. They require a hole in the cloth through which the barrel of the grommet passes. The setting of a grommet is similar to that of a hollow rivet and inexpensive tools are available which make an easy job of it. Extra layers of cloth are usually placed where the grommet is to be located to reinforce the area and distribute the strain. Lock stitches are used to attach the cloth reinforcement pieces before the grommet is inserted and set.

Loose grommets should be replaced or sewn, and sewing is simple. A round stitch is used, the lashing being passed through the grommet opening and cloth near the outer edge of the grommet, as illustrated in Figure 8. Note that the length of the stitches is staggered outside the grommet to distribute strain. A sewn grommet is much stronger than one merely peened in place and will rarely tear out. Be sure the grommet is somewhat larger inside than the diameter of the line which is to pass through it since the heavy thread used will reduce the clearance.

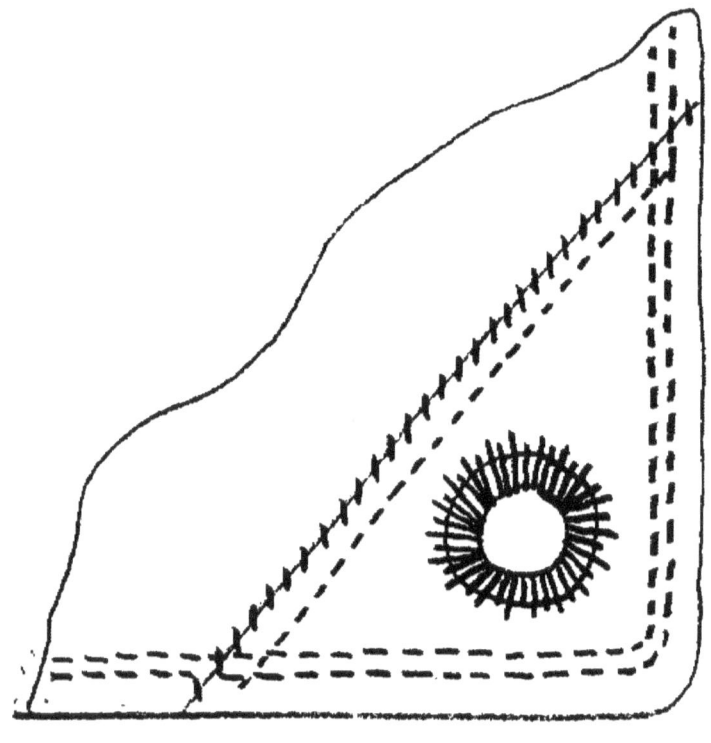

Figure 8

Sewn Grommet.

Modern standing rigging is made of twisted stainless steel wire cable or rods, which is best, or galvanized, cable which is nearly as long lasting if the galvanizing was correctly done. However, the elasticity of zinc and steel differ and the zinc coating on galvanized steel cable tends to flake off where the cable is bent sharply to go around a thimble. Rust at these points indicates a weakened cable which could part under strain and allow the mast to be carried over the side, bent, or broken. Wire cable designated as "1 x 19," meaning the cable is made of 19 separate strands of wire twisted together, is the strongest for its weight of the several configurations available. It must be of a diameter suited to the length of the mast and the sail area carried.

All wire and rod rigging should be periodically wiped with an oily rag to keep water from penetrating and corrosion from weakening the rigging. Rigging must be repaired or replaced whenever one or more broken strands are noted. Cared for properly, wire rigging should last approximately eight years on a boat used the year round.

When a shroud or stay requires replacement it is better to replace it in its entirety. However, temporary, repairs can be made if necessary by cutting out the damaged section and adding a new length of cable. Thimbles should be used to join wire cables and either an eye splice or cable clamp used to secure running ends to the standing parts of the cable near the thimbles.

Eye splices may be made similarly to those made in twisted line, but this is somewhat complex and difficult due to the stiffness of individual wires comprising the cable. A strong but much simpler tapered eye splice for rigging wire is illustrated in Figure 9.

To make the eye splice illustrated in Figure 9, leave about eight inches of wire and after forming the wire cable closely around the thimble. Separate one wire strand of the running end back to the thimble and wrap it snugly around both parts of the cable, placing the turns close together. Form the end of this single wire with pliers so it does not protrude from the cable, or snip it off close to the cable at the end of the wrapping. Then separate a second wire back to the end of the first wire wrap. Wrap it around both parts of the cable as the first wire was wrapped. Continue separating and wrapping wires until the eye splice is complete and all wires in the loose cable end have been wrapped. This results in a strong, attractive, tapered splice. The splice should be wrapped with oiled marline with ends secured to prevent any cut wire ends from coming in contact with sails, lines, or your hands.

Turnbuckles should be secured with cotter pins or rings and threads should be kept lubricated to avoid corrosion. A silicone grease is best to use on these threads. Canvas covers of synthetic cloth sewn closely around each turnbuckle will keep water and salt out and greatly lengthen turnbuckle life. These covers can be made as open ended sleeves sewn with a round stitch. Ends should be wrapped with marline to close them and prevent the entry of water along cables. The sleeves should enclose the eye splices on cable and will protect them from corrosion as well.

It will occasionally be necessary to climb to the top of the mast to inspect or replace fittings, bulbs, etc., and as an elevated lookout. Ratlines on a pair of shrouds are very nautical as well as a practical means for going aloft. Ratlines should extend high enough to allow you to climb onto the spreaders and reach rigging fittings and lights atop the mast. They need be constructed on only one set of shrouds -- it is not necessary to have ratlines port and starboard.

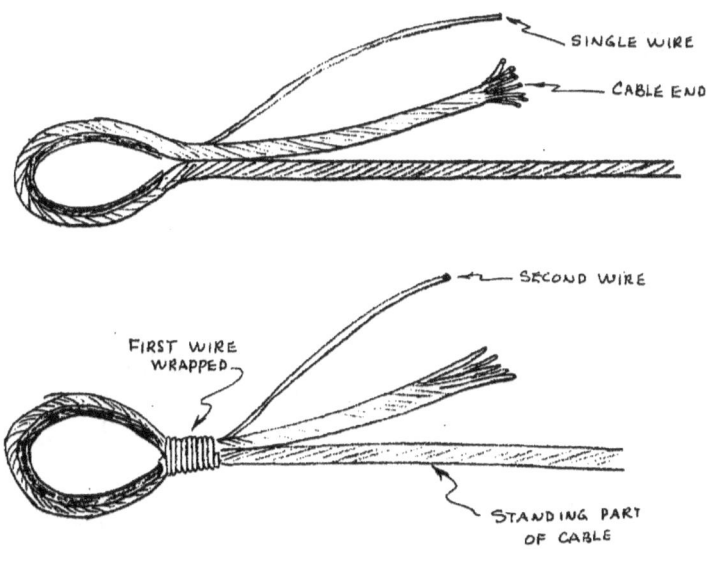

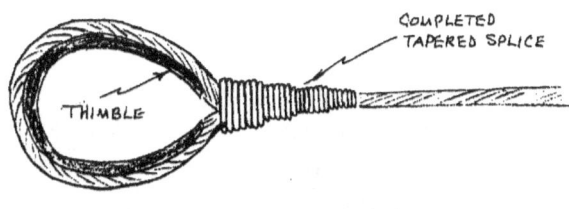

Figure 9

Wire Cable Eye Splice, Simplified.

Ratlines form a climbable ladder and rungs are usually placed about 18 inches apart. Rungs of metal, wood or rope may be used, and must be well secured to the shrouds so they will not slide down nor pull loose. Rope makes satisfactory ratlines and is easiest to secure to the shrouds, as illustrated in Figure 10. Use nylon or Dacron line 3/8-inch in diameter. Secure to each shroud with a clove hitch as shown, bringing the running end of each end of the hitch upward along the shroud. Lash well with marline as shown.

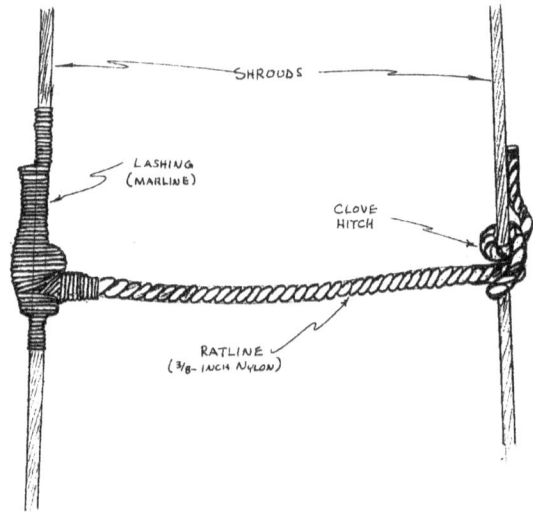

Figure 10

Ratlines.

A bosun's chair with two single block tackles is another method of going aloft, but can be somewhat more dangerous than ratlines. Use of a bosun's chair is not recommended to the inexperienced sailor since the chances of a fall are great unless the use of the chair is thoroughly understood. The main halyard, topping lift, or a separate block and line at the masthead may be used for hoisting. The pull must be from the tackle block if a 3:1 advantage is to be gained. If this block is at the masthead a length of hoisting line equal to three times the height of the mast will be required. The recommended system of tackle for hoisting the bosun's chair is diagrammed in Figure 11. Bosun's chair construction is illustrated in Figure 12, or a commercially available unit can be purchased.

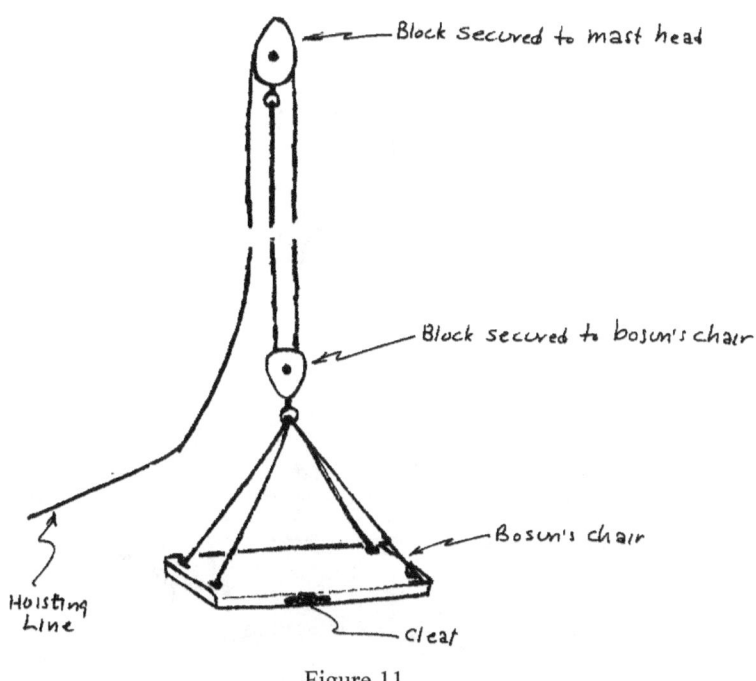

Figure 11

Bosun's Chair Hoisting Tackle.

Basic Boat Maintenance - - J. Frank Brumbaugh

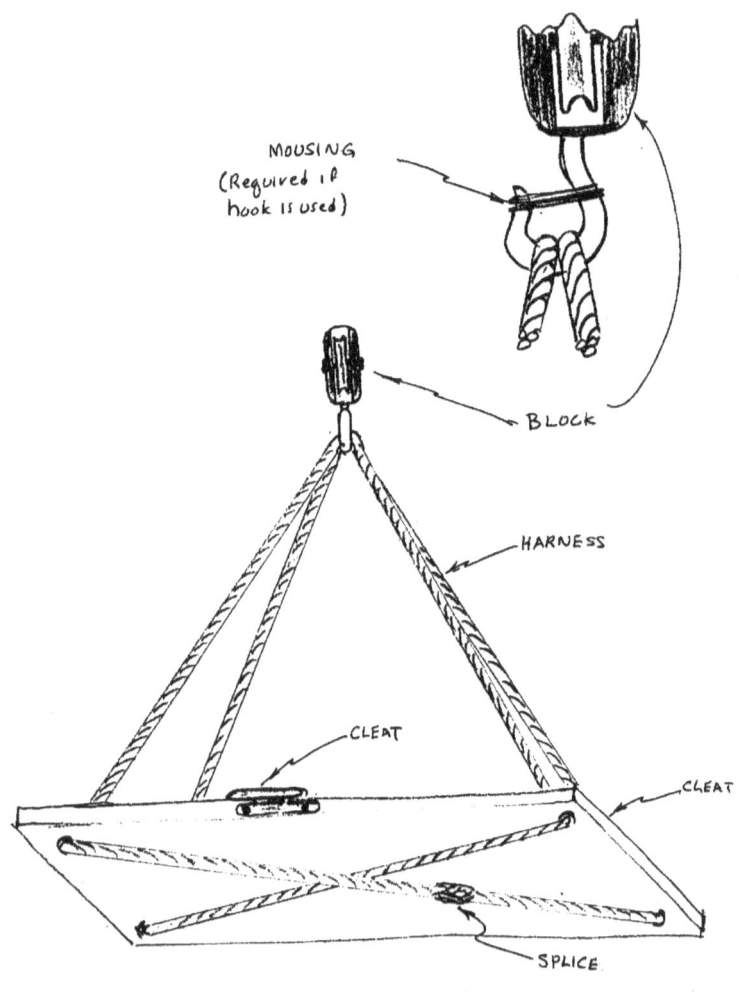

Figure 12

Bosun's Chair Construction.

A six by eighteen inch piece of hardwood an inch thick forms the seat of the bosun's chair. Teak is preferred. Marine plywood, oak, hickory or yellow pine completely without knots, splits or cracks is satisfactory. Three-eighths-inch diameter line is used for the harness and is crossed beneath the seat as shown in Figure 12. The harness line is spliced beneath the seat. The two sections of harness should be run through a ring fixed to a single tackle block or slung over a hook attached to the block. The hook must be moused with a lashing closing the hook opening to prevent the harness from accidentally slipping off the hook. A cleat must be attached to the seat of the bosun's chair to secure the running end of the hoisting line.

A foresail larger than 100 percent foretriangle, and occasionally the mainsail, may chafe against standing rigging and the spreader ends. Spreader ends should be padded with some soft material and covered with sewn canvas or taped to reduce sail chafe. Sails may be protected from chafing against standing rigging by covering shrouds with plastic hose or tubing eight or ten feet long. Tubing should be loose enough to rotate freely around the shrouds. Short lengths may be split for insertion between ratlines, and held together with waterproof plastic tape after installation. Plastic tubing may be required on lifelines forward, and the upper ends of stanchions may have to be padded and covered with canvas or plastic tape to protect the jib sail.

On sail boats, the backstay is often broken by insertion of egg insulators and used as a radio antenna. Insulators may be kept free of salt and moisture by wiping them with a light coating of silicone grease. Cracked or broken insulators must be replaced as soon as possible, as they may cause wide changes in the characteristics of the antenna. These changes can be reflected back to the radio transmitter, resulting in damage to the components. The backstay will be more efficient as an antenna if AWG 10 copper wire the same length as the backstay between insulators is connected at the upper end to the lead-in cable from the transmitter antenna connection, and the wire taped to the backstay at eight-inch intervals. The copper wire should be insulated or enameled except where connection is made to the lead-in at the upper insulator.

The system of lightning protection for the boat depends upon the certainty of grounding of all metal rigging, masts, and other large metal objects topsides to the underwater, radio ground plate. For additional protection, sizable metal parts within the hull should also be grounded into this network.

With proper grounding, an area within a cone having its apex at the highest grounded metal part, and with sides of 60 degrees, will be protected from lightning strikes. Sail boats with metal masts are easiest to protect. The mast and rigging are metallically connected together, and the lower ends of the rigging at the chain plates connected with AWG 8 copper wire, or copper strap or braid, to the radio ground plate on the hull. The engine, negative terminal of the battery and thus one side of the boat's wiring, and all other sizable metal constructions below decks are also connected to the radio ground plate. It will be preferable to mount a sharply pointed metal rod attached to the mast so it extends a few inches higher than the mast on a sail boat. This sharp point enhances the location of the cone of protection more than the normally blunt mast tip.

Motor-powered craft without tall masts are more difficult to protect, except those carrying lengthy metal whip-type radio antennas. The metal whip antenna can be used to provide a sizable cone of protection if care is taken to ensure proper grounding. Since most radio antennas have a coil connected in series with them, this coil must be bridged with a length of heavy copper wire or braid and the antenna connected to ground. With the antenna thus grounded for lightning protection, the boat's radio cannot be used. **Do not transmit into a grounded antenna!** This can cause serious damage to the radio and in some cases could start a fire. If the antenna is grounded but the coil is not bridged, the top of the cone of protection will be at the lowest point of the coil, not at the tip of the antenna as might be expected. This results from the peculiarities of lightning. Lightning will not pass through a coil or around a sharp corner, but will actually prefer to jump through the air to the nearest grounded metal. The technical explanation is the lightning waveform has an extremely sharp leading edge and thus will follow low impedance paths, but high impedance paths (such as coils of wire or sharp bends) appear as open circuits or very high resistances. If you don't understand the last sentence, don't worry about it. Be sure the path you provide for lightning is as straight and direct as possible. Any bends in this metallic path should be gradual, all connections made metal-to-metal, and all connections tight.

The metallic path provided for lightning protection will prevent lightning from striking your boat. It does not draw lightning, but is, in effect, a lightning rod such as is used to protect isolated buildings on land. It drains static electricity, which is present in the atmosphere preceding and during electrical storms, safely to ground. Thus prevents the potential between the clouds and your boat from rising high enough to cause lightning to strike.

Lifelines are usually constructed of plastic-covered wire cable, and require little maintenance. Where spliced to fittings at the ends where they connect to bow and stern pulpits, a little oil should be applied occasionally to the exposed metal to prevent corrosion.

Mounting hardware of pulpits and stanchions should be inspected periodically and tightened or replaced when necessary. Chromium, aluminum and stainless steel pulpits and stanchions should be washed free of salt and lightly oiled occasionally to keep them bright and free of corrosion.

Running rigging -- sheets, halyards, vang, outhauls, down hauls, etc. -- are usually of braided Dacron or flexible wire cable with Dacron tails. Three-eighths to half-inch braided Dacron line is more than adequate for boats 20 to 50 feet long. Running rigging should be swapped end for end whenever excessive wear appears where lines pass over sheaves. Lines badly worn at the ends can have the damaged portion cut away and the remainder used where its length is sufficient. Thus, old sheets and halyards can be pressed into service as vangs, downhauls and outhauls and other uses where the non-stretch qualities of Dacron are required. Running rigging of braided Dacron should last from four to eight years if properly cared for.

Be sure to tie a stopper knot -- a figure eight or an overhand knot -- in the running ends of halyards so they will not run entirely through the block if they are accidentally let go.

It will be advantageous to install an extra topping lift block at the mast head, fitted with a new halyard. This may be used in an emergency as a replacement for a broken topping lift, halyard, shroud or stay. It can be placed in service almost immediately when the need arises.

Ground tackle is extremely important to the boat which does not spend its lifetime tied to the dock. Even when the boat is taken out only occasionally it will pay to have proper ground tackle aboard and ready for use. Engines have been known to fail, and weather can change within minutes. You may have to anchor when you'd rather be safely at the dock but cannot get there for any of several reasons. Or you may want to anchor on a bright sunny day for a swim, or on a moonlit night for a party.

There is only one style of anchor that is

universally recommended for use on boats, where lightweight and ease of use are important. These are the patented lightweight anchors from *Fortress, Bruce, Danforth, CQR Plough* and *Nordhill*. These anchors bury easily, have extremely high holding power for their weight and size, and are easy to handle and retrieve.

Other types of anchors are occasionally used for special purposes and some are better suited to large ships rather than small craft.

The mushroom anchor is suitable only for permanent moorings and in large sizes weighing hundreds of pounds. They are not useful anchors for boats in sizes small enough to be picked up by one man.

The Kedge Anchor, the one most people picture when they hear the word anchor, is unhandy to stow, has little holding power for its weight, and is easy to foul because one fluke is always exposed.

The Stockless or Navy Anchor, the one seen drawn into hawse pipes on large ships, is a good anchor -- for large ships. It is little better than a concrete block in manageable sizes since it depends much on weight for holding power.

The grapnel, usually formed of five round, pointed flukes radiating from a stockless central shaft, is useful mainly in coral bottoms and for retrieving items lost over the side. It will be useful if you cruise over coral bottoms, and should weigh about as much as your working anchor.

Most boats which do any overnight or offshore cruising usually carry three anchors. A small, lightweight lunch hook for temporary, short term anchoring to prepare a meal or have a swim. A patented lightweight anchor of high-tensile steel, weighing five to ten pounds is suitable for boats 20 to 50 feet long. It is usually carried in the cockpit, lazarette or in chocks on deck where it can be rigged and tossed over the side when desired.

The working anchor -- the one used for overnight stops and anchoring in normal weather -- should always be rigged for immediate use. It may be in chocks on deck, lashed to the pulpit or in the rigging. A lightweight, high tensile patented anchor of 12 to 22 pounds is adequate for boats 20 to 50 feet long.

The third anchor is a storm anchor, used during heavy weather and where anchoring with two anchors may be desirable. It is usually stowed aft or below since there is always time to rig it when it is needed. A lightweight, high tensile patented anchor of 20 to 35 pounds is sufficient for boats 20 to 50 feet long.

A length of chain should always be used with any anchor. One to three fathoms of 1/4-inch to 7/16-inch chain is suggested for boats 20 to 50 feet long. The chain takes the chafe of rocks and shells on the bottom, protecting the fiber rode from damage, and keeping it generally clear of embedded sand. Boats habitually anchoring in rocks or coral often use chain for the entire anchor rode. However, chain is heavy, tends to rust, and a large amount of chain on board can cause unnoticed compass deviations. Chain in a locker forward can change the trim of the boat by making her bow heavy and possibly causing her to dive into the back of a wave, resulting in damage and possible pitch-poling. A swivel must always be used between anchor and an all-chain rode. Since swivels are weak points, they must be sufficiently large. A swivel will prevent chain rodes from kinking, but a swivel should never be used with all line rodes as it may cause hockles to form, badly weakening the line rode and possibly resulting in loss of the anchor.

Fiber anchor rodes should not be larger than necessary in diameter. Nylon lines 3/8-inch to 3/4-inch diameter are sufficient for boats 25 to 50 feet long. The value of nylon as an anchor rode is in its elasticity -- 14 percent for braided line and 25 percent for twisted nylon line -- and smaller diameter lines allow this elasticity to be more effectively used than larger diameter lines.

Braided nylon line is soft, easy to handle, and does not kink when fed into rope lockers. It is more complex to splice and does not have the elasticity of laid, twisted line. It is rapidly replacing twisted line on boats, not only as anchor rodes but for mooring and docking lines and for other miscellaneous purposes. It is also slightly more expensive than twisted line.

Twisted nylon line is familiar to all, relatively easy to handle, and coils well. It has more elasticity than braided line and is easier to splice. It is subject to twisting and hockles form easily. It is less expensive than braided line, but its reduced surface, a result of twisting, causes it to wear more rapidly and need replacement more often. Anchor rodes being used should be reversed end-for-end when wear is noted, usually at the end of a season to a year of use. Retired anchor rodes may be cut up and used for several more seasons for docking or mooring lines. One brand new rode should be carried for emergency replacement use on any long cruise.

Be sure the chain you buy is intended for anchoring, and is galvanized. Pretested chain costs only a little more and may save an anchor or your boat in a blow. If chain is to be used on a windlass, order calibrated chain. Short link chain may stretch and jam on the windlass. Stud link chain will not stretch, but it is heavier and the studs do not increase the strength of the chain.

An all-chain rode depends on its weight and the curve in the length of chain between Sampson post and anchor to absorb shock. This has the same results as the elastic stretching of a nylon fiber rode. Use a 25 or 50 pound weight as a rode rider to keep the rode on the bottom when the wind is gusty, especially when laying to chain on a short scope. Use a wide shackle on the weight so it will slide easily down the rode. A light line should be attached to the weight so it may be payed out and retrieved easily.

Be sure to always use sufficient scope when anchoring. A scope of five to eight times the water depth at your anchorage should be used if possible, the longer scope being used in heavier seas or windy weather. Since you will anchor in fairly shallow depths, a storm anchor rode of 300 feet and a service anchor rode of 200 feet are generally sufficient for boats up to 50 feet long.

Keep anchors, chain and line rodes clean and rust-free. Fiber rodes should be dry or nearly so before being fed below into the locker. Chain may be stowed wet in the chain locker if the bottom is fitted with a grating so water will drain into the bilge where it can later be pumped out. Lockers should also be well ventilated to prevent odors and mildew, although mildew will not affect the strength of nylon line.

Anchor rodes should be marked to determine how much is over the side. Marking every 25 or 50 feet is sufficient. Paint links on all chain rodes at the desired intervals. Feed strips of plastic beneath one strand of twisted line to mark intervals. Braided rodes can best be marked by wrapping colored, waterproof plastic tape around the line at the desired intervals.

Anchor flukes which become bent should be straightened by beating with a one or two pound machinist's hammer, using a block of wood or steel as an anvil. Anchors with bent flukes may not bury themselves properly in the bottom nor hold well and should not be trusted until repaired. Replacing the anchor is preferable, as the bending and straightening process will weaken the metal of the fluke. A bent fluke often indicates an anchor which is too light for the working load.

Basic Boat Maintenance - - J. Frank Brumbaugh

CHAPTER FOUR
ELECTRICAL SYSTEM

A neglected electrical system is a source of frustration, danger, and can even cause a fire. A comprehensive wiring diagram showing the location and function of every wire on the boat is one of the most essential documents for any boat owner. There should be no wires, switches or fuses whose function you do not know. The manufacturer of a new boat usually will supply such a diagram, but even if one is not available it will be relatively easy to trace out the wiring and make your own wiring diagram.

Every boat using electricity will have a switchboard, breaker panel or at least a group of switches mounted together with fuses for different circuits. All switches should be plainly labeled with their function; i.e., Running Lights, Radiotelephone, Cabin, etc. Fuses or breakers should be labeled with both their ampere rating and the circuit they protect.

Go over all the wiring in your boat, tracing each pair of wires between the power source and their destination. Insulation must be in good condition. Wires should not enter the bilges, except for power connections to electric bilge pumps, sump pumps, and high water alarms. All wiring should be as high in the boat as possible. Wires should be supported at 14-inch intervals with nonmetallic or insulated metal clips. There should be a little slack at the ends of all wires where they connect to terminals, lamp sockets, outlets, switches and fuses to allow for vibration and reconnection if breakage occurs at the connections. All connections should be tight. Screws are usually used to make connections at terminals. Crimp connectors with heat shrink tubing also suitable. Wire should be tinned stranded wire -- composed of a number of fine wires twisted together -- rather than a solid, single strand wire of large diameter wire (house wiring). Stranded wire is less subject to breakage caused by vibration than solid wire. All wire should be sufficiently large that there will be minimum voltage drop at the termination. Voltage drop -- reduced voltage -- is caused by resistance to the flow of electrical current and is inversely proportional to the cross-sectional area of the wires. Small diameter wire has higher resistance than large diameter wire.

    Table 5 gives wire sizes in AWG (American Wire Gage) numbers for various electrical loads in Amperes and for length of run for pairs of wires. These sizes are for DC circuits supplied by the boat's batteries. For AC circuits using shore power or an onboard motor-generator, the wire sizes needed are given in Table 6. The wire sizes given for AC circuits are sufficiently large for any normal length of run aboard boats to 50 feet or more in length.

    The lower the AWG number, the larger the wire diameter and the more current it can safely carry. An AWG number three gauges lower identifies a wire with twice the current carrying capacity. Most wiring on small boats need be no larger than AWG-10. Radiotelephones, radar and other high-amperage load devices will rarely require wire larger than AWG-8. Television sets draw less than two amperes at 12 VDC and well under one ampere at 32 VDC. Transistor radios draw so little current they can well be ignored when calculating loads to determine wire sizes and fuse ratings.

Electric hot plates, portable electric ovens, coffee makers, electric irons, heaters, etc., are not usually used on low voltage DC circuits supplied by the boat's batteries. These items would require so much current they would be impractical, discharging the batteries within a very short time. Most are made for use on shore power, 110-120 volts AC. Electric refrigerators operating from 12-volts or 32-volts DC are available but are practical only with the proper battery banks and charging system.

All circuits must be fused for safety. Fuses should be rated at somewhat more than the number of Amperes carried by each circuit, but never in excess of the number of Amperes which can safely be carried by the size wire used. Glass automobile-type fuses or breakers are normally used on boats for DC circuits. Fuses are readily available in boxes of five and are inexpensive and spare fuses of each value used should always be on board. Never, under any circumstances, replace a blown fuse with one having a higher ampere rating than the one being replaced. Fuses and breakers are protective devices -- insurance against damage, if you will -- and can only serve their purpose if properly used.

Circuit breakers, which act as combination switches and reusable fuses, are the standard on boats. They are not expensive and can be substituted for both switch and fuse in any circuit. Circuit breakers are manufactured in various ampere ratings, similar to fuses. If your boat is fully equipped with circuit breakers, you need carry no fuses since breakers provide the same protection and do not burn out.

WIRE USE CHART												
3% VOLTAGE DROP, 12VDC WIRING												
	LENGTH OF CONDUCTOR, SOURCE TO DEVICE & BACK TO SOURCE										
AMPS	10	15	20	25	30	40	50	60	70	80	100
5	16	16	14	12	12	10	10	10	8	8	6
10	14	12	10	10	10	8	6	6	6	6	4
15	12	10	10	8	8	6	6	6	4	4	2
20	10	10	8	6	6	6	4	4	2	2	2
25	10	8	6	6	6	4	4	2	2	2	1
30	10	8	6	6	4	4	2	2	1	1	0
40	8	6	6	4	4	2	2	1	0	0	2/0
50	6	6	4	4	2	2	1	0	2/0	2/0	3/0
60	6	4	4	2	2	1	0	2/0	3/0	3/0	4/0
70	6	4	2	2	1	0	2/0	3/0	3/0	4/0	
80	6	4	2	2	1	2/0	3/0	3/0	4/0	4/0	

Table 5

AC circuits use far fewer wire sizes since the voltage does not drop significantly in long runs.

15 amp circuits require 14 gauge wire.
20 amp circuits require 12 gauge wire.
30 amp circuits require 10 gauge wire.
50 amp circuits require 8 gauge wire.

Power driven boats use their engines often enough to keep batteries charged and make the use of electricity nearly as handy as ashore. Not so with sail boats. Electricity must be used sparingly on sail boats since the engine or genset must be run especially to recharge batteries. Lights and other electrical loads should be turned off when not in use to save the batteries, on all boats. It takes fuel to provide the horsepower to recharge batteries, and fuel is expensive. With diesel fuel, the cost may be less but the principle remains the same.

Wind-operated generators or alternators, and solar panels in different sizes and current capacities, are available for charging the boat's batteries. They are expensive and depending upon their mounting, can increase wind resistance in storm conditions. On most boats they can, over time, add charge to the batteries but none will produce much amperage under light wind conditions (for wind generators) and boat motion (for solar panels.)

The different types of electric light bulbs should be kept to a minimum. Often the same type number of bulb can be used throughout the cabin and for some of the navigation lights. Smaller bulbs used as a chart light, compass light and to illuminate lockers and enclosed spaces can often have the same type number. This reduces the number of different bulbs which must be carried as spares. Bulbs and their sockets should have two contacts on the base and have what is called a bayonet base; the bulb is inserted in the socket and given a partial clockwise turn to secure it, not screwed in as with a household bulb. Screw-base bulbs loosen under vibration and can fall out and break. They should not be used except for shore power or genset.

All exterior lights topsides must be sealed to prevent the ingress of moisture. The bulbs are usually enclosed behind a glass lens. Fresnel lenses are best since they concentrate the light horizontally and are thus much more efficient than clear glass lenses. Light bulbs with Fresnel lenses meet Inland and International Rules for visibility at lower current drains than those with clear glass lenses. This is particularly true for the starboard running light. There is no suitable bulb available for low voltage circuits which meets the requirements of the Rules for visibility of the starboard light with a clear lens, since green glass transmits only a small percentage of the light produced by the bulb.

For lazy skippers, an anchor light switch should be mounted near the head of the berth so the light can be extinguished at dawn without having to leave the coziness of the blankets. This can either be the only switch for the anchor light, or an extra switch may be wired in parallel with the normal anchor light switch. Connect a wire from one terminal on the berth switch to one terminal on the normal switch. Connect another wire between the remaining terminal on one switch to the remaining terminal on the other. With both switches off the anchor light will be controlled by either switch. With one switch on, the other switch will exert no control.

Bases of all bulbs and contacts inside all sockets must be kept bright and free of corrosion. Be sure the power is off before cleaning socket contacts with the tip of a screwdriver or a knife blade. Sand the bulb contacts lightly to remove dirt and corrosion.

Connections to lamps, switches, meters, fuses, etc., which are made with screws can be kept free of corrosion by a light application of silicone grease *(Dow-Corning DC-3* or *DC-4)* or a light oil after making sure connections are clean and tight. Soldered connections may be protected by oil, silicone grease, varnish, clear nail polish, etc.

Fuses should be removed periodically and their metal ends and the metal fuse clips sanded lightly to brighten them. Do not use oil or grease on electrical contacts.

Inspect all ground wiring. Ground wires, straps and braids do not require insulation, but all should be connected together and to the radio ground plate outside the hull. All connections should be scraped free of corrosion and made tight, with definite metal-to-metal contact. Lightning protection wiring is a part of the boat's grounding wiring system.

Keep all meters, fuse blocks, switchboards and junction boxes free of corrosion, dirt, oil and dust. All connections must be tight with bright, metal-to-metal contacts. There should be no play in wires or cables entering or leaving these locations but each wire should have an inch or two of slack between the last clamp or wire tie and the point to which it is connected.

Storage batteries are the heart of the boat's electrical system. They must be solidly mounted so they cannot shift in heavy seas under any foreseeable circumstances. They should be placed in a well ventilated spot low in the boat but not in the bilges where water could reach them. An acid-proof tray must be installed beneath the batteries to prevent spillage of electrolyte into the bilge and to prevent acid damage to the boat's structure. Fiberglass boats will not be harmed by accidental splashes of electrolyte.

Gel cell electrolyte is similar in consistency to candle wax and cannot be spilled. Gel cell batteries are sealed and can operate in any position. They can actually be operated under water if terminals and connections are sealed and waterproofed.

Gel cell batteries can be used as engine starting batteries as well as house batteries. They are deep cycle batteries and can be recharged fully even after having been completely discharged for as long as a month, without damage to the battery. However, no gel cell battery should be allowed to be discharged below 11

Volts, as measured by its charge level meter, and 11.5 Volts is a safer minimum. A fully charged 12 Volt gel cell battery will show a voltage of 12.9V. A fully discharged gel cell battery will show a voltage of only 10.5V.

The state of change of a gel cell battery is monitored using a special suppressed zero, expanded scale voltmeter, as described later in this chapter. A hydrometer, such as used to measure specific gravity of liquid electrolyte in common lead-acid batteries cannot be used with gel cell batteries, which do not contain liquid electrolyte.

Gel cell batteries must never be charged at greater than ten percent of the battery's ampere hour rate. Maximum charging voltage must not exceed 14.0 volts DC. When fully charged they may be maintained at 13.5 to 13.8 volts DC and the float current should be no more than a few hundred milliamperes (one milliampere equals one one-thousandth of an ampere).

The electrolyte in other than gel cell storage batteries consists of a mixture of sulfuric acid (H_2SO_4) and distilled water. Sulfuric acid spilled into salt water in the bilges generates chlorine gas, a very poisonous, heavier-than-air gas (used as a weapon's gas during World War I). Chlorine gas has also killed many aboard submarines when sea water entered the storage batteries through a leak in the hull during depth charge attack. Salt water and battery electrolyte must be kept apart. Only fresh water, preferably distilled, should be added to battery cells when necessary to keep the electrolyte at the proper level.

Batteries produce hydrogen gas while being charged. Hydrogen is not poisonous but is explosive. Being much lighter than air it will eagerly leave a properly ventilated compartment. Do not smoke or use open lights around storage batteries, and avoid causing electrical sparks. The chances are nothing drastic will happen -- but it could.

Batteries under charge also release water vapor, and eventually the amount of liquid in the cells is lowered as a result of this evaporation. Acid is not evaporated, only water. This is why water must occasionally be added to each cell. Acid or electrolyte should never be added to storage batteries after the initial filling of a dry-charged battery. Each different brand of battery has a specific level to which each cell should be filled with electrolyte at all times. This caution is usually marked on the battery in phrases such as, "Fill only to split ring," etc. The most important thing is never to allow the electrolyte level to fall so low the plates are exposed, as this can lower the capacity of the battery to supply power and greatly reduce its life. A weekly check of each cell in all batteries of both electrolyte level (add water if low) and specific gravity (recharge if low) and keeping a record with a battery log similar to that described in Figure 1 will ensure your batteries remain in top condition.

Storage batteries convert chemical energy to electrical energy while being used -- that is discharging -- and electrical energy to chemical energy while being charged. These actions cause changes in the specific gravity of the electrolyte, and allow a measurement of specific gravity to indicate the state of charge of the battery. The instrument used to measure specific gravity is called a *hydrometer*. (Do not confuse this with a *hygrometer*, an instrument used to measure relative humidity in the atmosphere.) It consists of a large diameter glass tube with a rubber bulb at the top and a short rubber hose at the bottom, and containing a weighted glass float which is calibrated in specific gravity and looks much like a swollen thermometer. See Figure 13.

NOTE: Be certain the hydrometer you use was made for lead-acid storage batteries and not for antifreeze specific gravity movement.

To measure specific gravity, squeeze the bulb and insert the hose into one cell of the battery. Release the bulb and draw enough electrolyte from the cell into the body of the hydrometer so the float is floating freely but is not jammed against the top of the hydrometer body. Read the specific gravity of the electrolyte at the calibration on the float which is at the level of electrolyte in the hydrometer. Log this value and replace the electrolyte in the same cell from which it was withdrawn by squeezing the bulb. A specific gravity of 1.280 (often called 1280) to 1.300 per cell is proper for a fully charged battery. A specific gravity of 1.110 is fully discharged. The specific gravity of 1.180 shown in Figure 13 indicates a partly discharged battery which should soon be charged to bring the specific gravity of the electrolyte back to normal for a fully charged battery.

The hydrometer should be kept in the battery compartment in padded clips which protect it from breakage. The hose should rest in a plastic or lead cup which will trap any drips and prevent them spilling.

Suppressed zero, expanded scale voltmeters are available commercially from some marine instrument manufacturers which can be switched across each battery in turn to give an accurate indication of its percentage of charge at a glance. These are expensive, specially designed voltmeters which spread out a range of five or six volts over most of the meter scale. This instrument operates on the principle that there is a very slight difference in the voltage of a fully charged battery from one which is only partly charged. By spreading out this

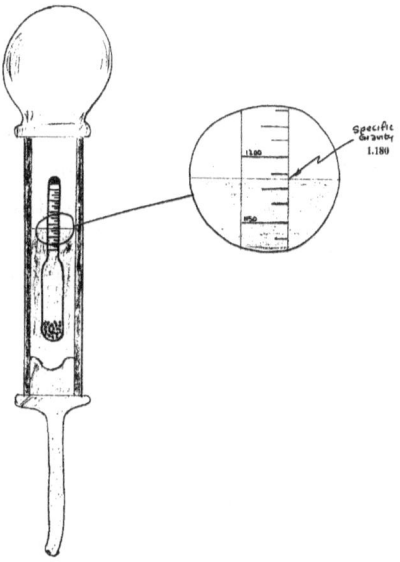

Figure 13

Hydrometer.

small voltage difference over two or more inches on the scale of a special voltmeter it is possible to gain an indication of the condition of the battery. These instruments complement but do not replace the hydrometer, except for gel cell batteries and they are automatic in use. Specific gravity should still be measured in each cell at least once a month if one of these meters is used. At the same time the electrolyte level should be checked and brought to the proper level with distilled water as required.

    Corrosion is the major enemy of batteries which otherwise are cared for properly. Tops of batteries and their cases should be wiped off each time the batteries are inspected. Use a wet cloth wrung out in a solution made with two teaspoons of baking soda to a quart of fresh water.

Corrosion appearing on battery terminals and connections looks like salt or sugar which has been dampened so it sticks together. Similar corrosion, green in color, may appear on exposed copper wires or cable. This corrosion must be removed to prevent metal parts from being eaten away. Loosen connections and scrape battery posts and the inside of their mating connectors with sandpaper or a knife blade until they are bright. Scrape all other corrosion away. Wash with baking soda and water solution, being extremely careful not to allow any of this solution to get inside the cells. Dry thoroughly, replace connections and tighten well. Cover all exposed metal parts of battery connections and cables with silicone grease *(Dow-Corning DC-3* or *DC-4)* or petroleum jelly such as *Vaseline*. Silicone grease will not melt off and, if properly applied to clean metal surfaces, will prevent corrosion for the life of the battery. Petroleum jelly will last only a week or two before it must be reapplied. A one-ounce tube of silicone grease is more than enough for all the batteries on a 50-footer. The coating need not be more than 1/32-inch thick but it must be thorough.

There should be a master switch connected between the batteries and all current-using loads which, when opened (turned off), removes power from all electrical items on board. One exception to this is the automatic bilge pump. This must be wired so power is always available to the pump in case the water in the bilge rises while no one is aboard. Another possible exception is a fire/burglar alarm to protect the boat while it is unmanned. Power to all other equipment must be interrupted when the master switch is off.

CHAPTER FIVE
GALLEY, HEAD, AND PLUMBING

The galley is where a happy or unhappy cruise is made. It must be maintained shipshape and in Bristol fashion always. A very good rule to remember -- and follow -- is: "Never put anything **down**. Put it **back**!" Then you will always know exactly where everything is located. Dirty dishes and cooking utensils must be washed and replaced in their racks or lockers and never allowed to pile up. The stove must be kept clean and its fuel tank full. The drip pan beneath the stove must never be allowed to become a catchall for grease, food scraps and burned matches. Pumps must be clean and in operating condition. The sink must be kept clean and odor-free as must the ice box or refrigerator. The gash bucket must be emptied regularly, long before it threatens to overflow. No plastic may ever be discarded into the water. Stores must be properly stowed, easy to reach and some control applied so you are never out of something you thought sure you had. Counters and tables must be kept clean and free of clutter. Spills must be cleaned up as they occur. Every crumb, every scrap of food not eaten must find its way into the gash bucket and not allowed to become food for insects. It will also help if there is someone aboard who knows how to cook and -- hopefully -- enjoys doing so. The galley in a small boat is usually small and compact, and laid out with some attention to the problems of preparing and serving meals where nothing is level except momentarily and accidentally. "One hand for the ship and one hand for the sailor," is excellent advice for the cook. He should be able to brace himself in one spot, perhaps even sitting down on the companionway ladder, and function efficiently without having to move. Everything he needs should be arranged so it is within reach. This may take some doing but the results will be well worth it.

The stove is perhaps the most important single item in the galley next to food. Most boats are equipped with a two-burner stove which burns alcohol under pressure. Some use kerosene-burning *Primus* stoves. A number cook with bottled gas. A few even have electric ranges with ovens. And there are a few older boats which use wood, charcoal or coal for cooking fuel.

The alcohol stove is the safest since alcohol fires can be extinguished with water. They are a bit tricky to prime, sometimes flare up, do not work well with flames set low. The fuel, denatured alcohol, is rather expensive and not readily available outside United States waters.

Non-pressurized alcohol stoves, such as the popular ORIGO stoves made in Sweden, are safer and much easier to use than any pressurized stoves. They cannot flare up nor spill fuel. The alcohol is contained in fiber-filled stainless steel containers with a wire grill over the opening. Each holds over a quart of alcohol. Only the alcohol vapor burns; no free liquid alcohol is present. Flame is easily controlled from low to high by stainless steel vanes moved over the burner by a plastic handle in front of each burner. Each burner will bring a quart of water to a boil in a few minutes. Used on high flame, each burner will use about a quart of alcohol in 6 to 7 hours. Fuel lasts much longer at normal lower cooking settings.

Primus stoves, made mostly in Sweden but available all over the world, burn kerosene under pressure. *Optimus* is the brand most often used today. They are the most dependable of all stoves and as safe as alcohol stoves if care is taken in their use. *Primus* stoves have been the choice of Arctic and Antarctic expeditions, have been taken to the top of Mount Everest, have operated dependably all over the world and in all climates. Kerosene is the least expensive of all liquid fuels suitable for use aboard ship. It is available in even the most remote parts of the globe. Flame is controlled more readily than pressurized alcohol stoves and they operate well at low flame settings. *Primus* stoves require priming with alcohol, however, although two gallons of alcohol will be more than sufficient for a full year's priming of a two-burner *Primus* stove used every day to prepare complete meals.

Bottled gas stoves are easy to use, clean, and quick cooking. They are as convenient as any kitchen gas range. They require no priming and fuel is reduced to a pressurized gas when it leaves the tank. Tanks must be mounted on deck outside the cabin. A combination of flexible rubber gas lines copper tubing with tight, flared fittings connected between pressure regulator and the stove. Tanks may explode if they get too hot and if the safety valve does not release. Leaking propane or butane gas, like gasoline vapor, is heavier than air and can seep into the bilges. This is an explosive mixture which can be set off by a spark and is as potentially dangerous as a cargo of dynamite. Properly maintained and used, a bottled gas system can be safe, and installations are often seen on boats longer than 30 feet. Bottled gas is available outside United States waters but tanks, fittings, and pipe threads vary in other countries.

Electric ranges are suitable only on larger boats over which remain dockside, connected to shore power or carry generators aboard to provide electricity for the stove.

Wood, coal and charcoal are used for cooking on very few pleasure boats. They are safe in that there is no explosive danger, but they are hot, slow to use, and the fuel is dirty, bulky, and heavy. A charcoal Hibachi for use on the beach or in the cockpit when anchored or docked will allow a change of pace in the cooking department, but will not replace a proper stove.

Every stove must have sea rails to prevent pots from sliding off and dumping their contents. The best are adjustable to the size pot on each burner. Pot clamps or springs with hooks at each end hold pots firmly down against the burner. Bronze wool or stainless steel wool should be used to keep rails, clamps and the stove proper clean and shiny. Spilled food should be wiped off before it bakes or burns into a hard crust difficult to remove.

A drip pan must be installed beneath the stove. It serves to catch spilled fuel, food and burned matches accidentally dropped through the burners. It should be wiped out after each meal at the same time the stove is cleaned. Hot water and detergent or a rag or sponge will suffice for most cleaning.

Stove burners must be kept clean. Scrape burned grease off and clean with bronze or stainless steel wool, with or without detergent and water, as desired. Generators, on stoves so equipped, must be kept clean. A wire of suitable diameter run through the orifice will keep it open. One spare generator should be carried on long cruises.

Stoves are sometimes mounted in gimbals, especially on sail boats. Gimballed stoves remain level under conditions of heel but they require much room and the weight necessary for stability is unnecessarily heavy. Gimballed and half-gimballed stoves, by calling attention to the motion of the boat, often contribute to the onset of seasickness for anyone below decks. Gimbals must be kept lubricated so they will operate freely without binding and to prevent squeaks.

Mounting hardware and screws holding fuel control knobs must be checked periodically and tightened or replaced when necessary.

The fuel line and connections must be checked for leaks. Soapy water applied over connections of bottled gas fuel lines will bubble if any gas is leaking. Fuel lines for alcohol and kerosene stoves may be checked for leaks by passing a piece of toilet tissue along the line and around each connection. Dampness on the tissue indicates a leak. Fuel lines between the stove and separate fuel tank must be firmly supported with padded metal clips. A line several feet long must have an expansion loop within its span, or it may be shaped so a complete circle of tubing is formed midway along the span to absorb expansion. Flexible fuel tubing to gimballed stoves must be carefully checked for leaks and replaced immediately if a leak is noted. Most leaks at fittings on copper tubing fuel lines can be stopped by tightening the fitting with a pair of wrenches. Always use two wrenches to prevent twisting the tubing or wringing it off.

A shutoff valve at the fuel tank should be accessible even if the stove itself is in flames.

There should be a dry chemical or carbon dioxide fire extinguisher within immediate reach of the cook but not too near the stove which is the source of most galley fires. Dry chemical is better than carbon dioxide for grease fires but it does leave a mess to clean up and ruins food it touches, while carbon dioxide does neither. Alcohol fires are best extinguished with water or damp cloths. An old plastic cleanser container with sprinkle top, filled with a mixture of half and half table salt and baking soda is handier, less expensive and often easier to use to extinguish grease fires than a dry chemical fire extinguisher. The contents of both are similar, and the homemade sprinkle extinguisher can be recharged in the galley at little expense.

The galley sink is seldom used as a sink at sea, but it makes a fine place to stow needed small items. Dishes and cooking utensils are best washed in a bucket of sea water on deck or in the cockpit when at sea. This is not only easier, it keeps from making a mess in the galley. Liquid detergents like Joy and Lux Liquid lather well in salt water. When docked and where city water is available, dish washing can be done at the sink or in a bucket, whichever seems handier. The sink must be kept clean and dry at all times. Grease, food particles and moisture are attractive to insects.

Install a good quality mirror, preferably of plate glass laminated to plywood in the galley, unless the head is large enough to contain a wash basin. Personal grooming is accomplished at the galley sink when the head is not available or not equipped for this purpose. The mirror should be eight inches by ten inches or larger if it is to be useful.

Paper towels will be extremely handy for wipe-ups in the galley. However, they take up much space. A better idea is to keep a roll of toilet tissue in the galley for this purpose. It is best stowed on a tissue rack but may be hidden in a locker if its presence in the galley seems incongruous.

Water and sump pumps in the galley are very dependable. They should be disassembled periodically, especially before leaving on an extended cruise, and the interior parts inspected. Ragged pump leathers and worn or cracked O-rings and impellers should be replaced when noticed, and these items should be carried as a part of normal spares. Follow the pump manufacturer's recommendations for lubrication of pumps. Salt water pumps must be operated every day, even while in port, or they will become slimy and odorous from the growth of marine bacteria.

Inspect fresh and salt water lines and drains. Connections must be kept tight to prevent leaks. Lines must be supported at intervals with metal or plastic clamps so vibration can not cause leaks or damage. Long runs of copper tubing must contain an expansion loop as described previously for stove fuel lines. Plastic tubing must be inspected for checks and cracks and be replaced when necessary. Cable clamps must be kept tight. Seacocks should be operated periodically to keep their operating parts from being frozen open or closed by marine growths or corrosion. Inoperable seacocks must be replaced as soon as possible, no later than the next time the boat is careened or hauled.

Clear plastic tubing used for water lines will soon become cloudy and have a slimy deposit on the inner surface. This is caused by the growth of harmless bacteria and is not a cause for any concern unless the water develops an off taste or mustiness. Water tanks and hoses can be sweetened when required if there is a convenient source of fresh water nearby. Mix four ounces of baking soda in water and add to the water tank which must then be filled. This water should remain in the tank for 24 hours. A few hours sail will agitate the water inside the tank sufficiently so all interior surfaces will be well wetted. Pump all the water from the tank through the galley pump and overboard through the sink drain. Refill the tank with fresh water and again pump it all overboard through the galley sink. The tank and water lines should now be sweet and clean and the tank should be refilled with fresh water. The water will be free of objectionable taste and odor.

If the fresh water you must place in your tanks comes from a source of questionable purity, you can easily make it safe to drink by chlorinating it much the same as is done ashore for municipal water supplies. Any chlorine containing household bleach such as *Clorox* or similar liquid bleach should be added to the fresh water tank at a rate of two teaspoons to each ten gallons of water. Ordinary Tincture of Iodine, available at most drug stores, may also be used in half the amounts specified for bleach. The water will be safe to drink after standing several hours or over night. The first amount pumped out, equal to the line volume from the tank to the faucet, should be discarded since it effectively sterilizes the water line and pump. Water purified in this way in portable jugs which can be shaken to mix well will be safe to drink within one hour. The additional time specified for tanks allows complete decontamination in the absence of shaking the contents for thorough mixing. Fresh water from wells, streams and similar sources in areas where flukes are present (Puerto Rico, South Pacific, Asia, Africa, etc.) must not be used for drinking until at least 48 hours after filling the tanks, regardless of the purification system used. Blood and liver flukes are invisible to the eye during that stage of growth spent in fresh water. Their life cycle requires them to spend a part of their life as an internal parasite of fresh water snails and part as an internal parasite in men. Flukes are dangerous and a fluke infestation is painful and difficult to cure. However, avoidance of this danger is simple since flukes must enter man within a few hours after leaving the body of a snail or they will die. Forty-eight hours standing will render water completely free of live flukes, and this period includes a wide safety margin which is more than sufficient in all cases.

  Dishes, mugs, tumblers, cutlery, spices and condiments are usually stowed in specially designed racks, in which they should be kept at all times when not in use. Thin cork or felt is used to provide protection against breakage and eliminates rattles between the racks and their contents. *Melmac* or similar plastic is best for dishes. Mugs and tumblers should be of plastic, and those with double walls (called *thermal)* will keep their contents hot or cold for longer periods. Tableware and cooking utensils are best made of stainless steel. Pots and pans of stainless steel with copper bottoms are best, but heavy aluminum will serve nearly as well. All should be equipped with lids.

    A four-quart cast aluminum pressure cooker with rack and vegetable pans will be extremely useful as it saves fuel by cooking quickly. It also saves time since several foods may be cooked in it at the same time without any mixing of flavors. It can also be used for baking bread. The pressure cooker will not spill its contents even if it is thrown to the deck by a jibe, a sudden gust or heavy sea. A small dish drain will be handy for stowing small objects and also for carrying food topsides while under way.

    A deep, cast aluminum or cast iron skillet with cover, called a "chicken fryer," is not only useful for frying and pan roasting but, if equipped with a wire rack, can be used as an oven for top-of-the-stove baking of bread, rolls, biscuits, cookies, cakes and pies. A folding oven with temperature gauge in the door which fits over one burner of the galley stove is also useful for baking. *Coleman* produces a suitable folding oven. Detergent and sea water -- or fresh water when it is available in unlimited quantities -- is used for pan and dish washing. A bucket in the cockpit will be more convenient than the galley sink when at sea. Use only bronze mesh, stainless steel wool or plastic scrubbers in the galley. Ordinary steel wool, *Brillo* soap pads and similar scrubbing aids will rust badly, causing stains, and should never be taken aboard.

    Lengths of bungee or shock cord should be

installed across all locker openings to restrain contents when locker doors are open. Shock cord is also valuable for restraining any loose objects which might shift in a seaway.

Stores of food should be carefully inventoried and a record kept of where each is stowed. Dry foods such as flour, sugar, oatmeal, dry beans, etc., should be kept in airtight plastic containers. Clean half-gallon plastic milk containers make excellent air- and moisture-proof containers for dry staple foods such as dry beans, split peas, pasta, oatmeal, rice, sugar, salt, flour, etc. They also will keep insects at bay. A funnel cut from the top of a 2-liter plastic soda bottle makes filling the milk containers very easy. Salt must be kept in a plastic container as it will corrode metal. Foods purchased in boxes or bags should be transferred to plastic containers to protect them from dampness and keep them fresh longer. Canned goods should be marked on one end with their contents, using a felt tipped marker containing waterproof ink. If stored in the bilges, paper labels should then be removed to prevent their loosening due to moisture and clogging limber holes, bilge pumps, or a sodden mess in the bilge. Do not stow cans where there is a likelihood of their coming in contact with water. Table 7 gives the storage life of a number of common foods.

Slab bacon and chunk cheese can be prevented from molding by keeping them wrapped in cheesecloth which has been dipped in vinegar and then wrung out. Mold spots may be scraped or cut off and the remainder of the bacon or cheese used normally.

Fresh eggs can be stored for up to three months if the shells are first wiped with a cloth dipped in mineral oil, available at any drug store. Eggs can also be prepared for storage by immersing them in boiling water for five seconds. Eggs should be stored in a dark, cool place.

TABLE 7
STORAGE LIFE OF COMMONLY USED FOODS

FOOD PRODUCT	SHELF LIFE IN MONTHS*
Milk, evaporated	6
Milk, dry, in metal or plastic airtight container	6
Canned meats	18
Canned fish (sardines, salmon, kippers, etc.)	12
Mixed meat and vegetable (stew, chile, hash, soup)	18
Condensed soup, canned	8
Berries, sour cherries, canned	6
Citrus fruit juices, cans or bottles	6
Other fruits and juices, canned (peaches, pears, apples, etc.)	18
Dry fruit in metal or plastic airtight container	6
Tomatoes, sauerkraut, canned	6
Other vegetable, canned	18
Dry beans, peas, in airtight containers	18
Dry cereal in metal or plastic airtight container	12
Dry cereal in original cardboard box	1
Oatmeal in airtight metal or plastic container	24
Oatmeal in original cardboard box	12
Flour in airtight metal or plastic container	12
Hydrogenated fats (canned shortening)	12
Sugar in moisture-proof container	Indefinite
Hard candy, boiled sweets, chewing gum	18
Nuts, shelled and canned	12
Puddings, brown bread, date and nut bread, canned	12
Coffee, tea, cocoa, in airtight containers	18
Dry cream substitute in airtight containers	12
Boullion cubes in airtight container	12
Beverage powders in airtight containers	24
Salt	Indefinite
Baking soda, baking powder, dry yeast in airtight container	12
Spices	24

*Average. Foods should be rotated and consumed within these time limits to prevent deterioration in taste and nutritive quality.

Smithfield hams, and other brands which have been smoke cured, store well without refrigeration, as do certain types of sausage. Any similar preserved meat which is not kept in a refrigerated counter in the store can be relied upon to store well without spoiling and without refrigeration on your boat.

Sliced, fresh tomatoes immersed in an oil-and-vinegar salad dressing and stowed in airtight containers will remain edible for months.

Potatoes should be stored in a cool, dark, well ventilated area. Onions should be stored in the light, in mesh bags. Check fresh vegetables in storage frequently and discard any showing signs of rot. The odorous, slimy mess made by rotting potatoes and onions must be experienced to be believed.

Citrus fruits and bananas should be purchased green if they are to be kept aboard for more than a few days. They should be stowed in a cool, dark place, and placed on deck in the sun to ripen as required. Lime and lemon juice is available in glass bottles and will find many uses aboard in beverages, cooking, and as a sauce for seafood. Ice boxes and electrical refrigerators should be cleaned weekly while in use. Wipe out with a cloth or sponge dipped in a solution of two teaspoons of baking soda and one quart of fresh water. Discard spoiled or moldy food whenever noted. A cup of used but dry coffee grounds in a paper cup or foil container will keep the ice box odor free. So will an open box of baking soda.

Ice boxes should be cleaned as described above and dried well when on a cruise and no ice is available. The door or lid should be cracked open for ventilation. An empty icebox can be used to stow dry foodstuffs and other items when it is not being used for cooling fresh food with ice. Drains must be kept clear and hoses should be inspected for cracks or leaks and replaced if necessary. Dry rot in wood hulls often starts behind or beneath ice boxes where ventilation is poor and where fresh water may accumulate. All ice boxes should drain over the side and never into the bilge where they can cause odors, and may also cause rot in wood boats. Where the ice box drain is below the waterline as on many sail boats, a sump and pump may be used to discharge water from melting ice. As a substitute, a removable but well secured drip pan can be used to catch the water from the ice compartment. The pan must be dumped over the side regularly to prevent its overflowing and draining into the bilges.

The head should be kept clean by proper use and

flushing, and given special attention weekly. Household bleach or commercial bowl cleaners should be applied to bowls weekly to remove stains. Ask the manufacturer of your head to recommend commercial cleaning products which will not damage the bowl, gaskets, and other components. Wipe off the outside of the bowl frequently. Brass or bronze fittings should either be kept shined with metal polish or be cleaned with bronze or stainless steel wool and kept lightly oiled to prevent corrosion. *Lysol* spray deodorant is excellent for eliminating odors in the head.

The Y-valve must be set to conduct waste from the head into the holding tank when in US waters. It is illegal to discharge waste overboard except in international waters, or in the territorial waters of countries allowing such discharge.

Holding tanks may be pumped out only in marinas and ports where pump-out facilities are located. Even in countries where overboard discharge of waste from the head is allowed, it is only common courtesy to not discharge such waste in harbors, marinas, moorings, or anchorages.

Seacocks not normally operated each time the head is flushed should be operated weekly to keep them in functioning condition. Seacocks on water inlet and drains in the head should always be kept closed when the head is not in use. When the head is below the waterline as is true of most sail boats and many large power boats, a sea cock inadvertently left open can sink an unattended boat.

Be certain gaskets and valves are in good condition and all hardware is tight. A spare joker valve and set of gaskets should be maintained as a part of normal spares carried, especially on a long cruise.

Marine heads contain constricted passages, small diameter pipes and carefully fitted valves. Properly used they will continue to give good service for many years with little attention. However, they are easy to stop up and clearing the stoppage generally means dismantling the head, a thankless job at any time and especially trying when at sea. *Do not put anything into the head unless you've eaten it first!* This is important. The head is not a garbage disposal nor can it handle such things as sanitary napkins, tampons, filter tip cigarette butts, match sticks, orange peels, apple cores, paper towels, bobby pins, and the many similar objects deftly assimilated by most toilet bowls ashore.

When a manual head is used, operation will be easier and flushing more thorough if a double sheet of toilet tissue is first laid over the brass valve in the bottom of the bowl. To flush, pump water into the bowl before opening the outlet valve, then pump into the holding tank, or overboard if at sea, admitting water and pumping until all wastes are gone and the interior of the bowl is clean.

Showers, bathtubs and wash basins must be kept clean with detergent and water. Scouring powder should not be used unless the equipment manufacturer states it's safe to use. All should be flushed with clean water (usually sea water) after use and after each cleaning. Water and sump pumps should be inspected periodically and damaged leathers, O-rings and impellers replaced. Lubricate as recommended by the pump manufacturer. Keep seacocks closed on all fixtures installed below the waterline. Operate seacocks weekly to keep them operable longer.

A holder for toilet tissue should be installed in the head. Do not use dime store metal fittings since they are subject to rust. Plastic holders are satisfactory, but be sure to buy a sturdy one and install it securely. Towel rings are better than towel bars which usually manage to deposit the towel on the deck while underway. Hooks may be used but should be rustproof and installed high to prevent injury.

In heads large enough to contain a wash basin, a mirror should also be installed. This can be a full length mirror on the inner surface of the door, the front of a medicine cabinet or a small (8" x 10" or larger) plate glass mirror laminated to plywood and mounted at a suitable height above the wash basin. Mirrors can be cleaned with detergent and fresh water and polished with tissue or paper towels, or one of the commercial glass cleaners may be used. A tissue dampened with alcohol is a good cleaner for mirrors and glass.

Chrome plated fittings should be kept clean and shiny. Metal polish, alcohol on a tissue, or detergent and water will keep them looking bright.

The "medicine cabinet," if present, should be fitted with a door which latches securely. Sea rails or lengths of shock cord should be installed along the front of each shelf to prevent contents from spilling out. The shelves should also have lips or fiddles along the front. Contents should be limited to toilet articles, cosmetics and such items as aspirin, antacid tablets, antiseptic, adhesive bandages and prescription drugs normally taken daily. First aid and medical supplies, medicines and drugs should be stowed separately and will be considered in the next chapter. Aspirins should be discarded when they develop a strong vinegar odor and become crumbly. Outdated or no longer needed prescription drugs should be discarded.

CHAPTER SIX
BELOW DECKS, FURNISHINGS, AND SPARES

Your boat's cabin should be a comfortable, snug and cozy place during heavy weather, yet be airy and bright when the weather is fine. Since most, if not all furniture, will be built-in, you will be limited to making the most of what was initially installed by the builder.

Ventilation is most important to prevent dampness, clamminess and musty odors or mildew. Hatches and the main companionway should be kept open whenever the weather allows and someone is on board. Aside from these, most boats are equipped with small ventilators which aid in exhausting stale air and bringing fresh air into the cabin. Ports and windows can often be at least partly open even when it is raining. Fans and blowers can be used, particularly when the boat is at rest in inclement weather. Air conditioners, if available, are valued during hot, humid weather.

Ventilation may become a problem during summer rains when several persons are confined below decks. All ventilators and ventilated hatches must be constructed so air may enter freely but rain and spray are excluded. Bronze or fiberglass screens over ventilator and hatch openings will prevent insects and rodents from coming below.

The main companionway hatch, doors or washboards can usually remain open regardless of weather or spray if an awning or spray shield is rigged to protect this opening. A wind sail rigged to direct air through the open forward hatch will be appreciated at anchor or underway in quiet waters in hot weather.

Interiors should be kept painted or waxed so they will remain clean and airy in appearance. Windows, ports and deadlights should be kept clean and free of salt encrustation. Slightly off-white or very light colors should be used on bulkheads and overheads to give the illusion of spaciousness. Carlins, cabin beams and wood trim may be teak, varnished wood or painted in a dark, contrasting color. Varnished surfaces require removal of varnish, sanding and revarnishing at intervals. Fiberglass and painted wood surfaces should be washed and waxed. Use a paste type automobile wax or a wax manufactured especially for fiberglass, for the annual or semiannual waxing. A product like *Bon-Ami Dust n' Wax* or equivalent should be used occasionally to keep the surface clean and shining between paste waxing. Mildew may attack painted surfaces and looks like sprinkles and patches of soot. It can be removed by washing with a solution of one cup household liquid bleach and a half gallon of fresh water. Use rubber gloves since this solution may be irritating to the skin. When dry, apply wax over the cleaned portion if the interior is waxed.

All tables, cabinet or counter tops and the exposed tops of lockers must be surrounded by sea rails or fiddles to contain objects placed on them. Fiddles should have openings at least at the corners so the surface may be cleaned more easily and crumbs and other small bits of debris removed. Wax should be applied regularly to plastic and *Formica* countertops. Particular attention must be paid to prevent thick encrustations of wax where tops meet fiddles or bulkheads. If a hardwood cutting board is installed as a part of the ice box top or counter top, it should never be waxed. Wash and rinse well after each use, blot dry and leave exposed to air. After it is completely dry, a light coating of vegetable or mineral oil should be applied.

Hardware fastenings, catches, hinges and knobs on drawers, lockers, compartments and folding tables or table leaves should be regularly inspected. Corrosion should be removed, screws and bolts tightened or replaced and hinges, catches and other moving parts lubricated as necessary.

All shelves should have lips and their contents protected by sea rails. Shock cord can be used in place of solid sea rails to make insertion and removal of objects on the shelves easier. This is particularly applicable to book shelves.

Lockers, drawers, compartments and all enclosed spaces must be well ventilated to prevent mildew or other damage to their contents. Drawers may be vented by cutting slots through their fronts for use instead of knobs or handles. Drawers should be self-locking when closed, and preferably the front of drawers should require lifting a fraction of an inch before they can be opened. Locker doors and compartments can be ventilated by holes, slots or cutouts placed near the top and bottom. Lockers also are often ventilated by doors made of a frame supporting cane, mesh or woven strips of wood. All of these are attractive, light in weight and provide excellent ventilation. Since most boat cabins encompass restricted space, anything which gives the feeling of openness will be appreciated on dark, blustery days when you are forced to stay below. Light colors on bulkheads and the overhead help, as mentioned previously. Mirrors make the cabin appear very spacious, increase the light and will be much appreciated by any ladies aboard. A full length mirror on the main cabin side of the door closing off the forward cabin adds greatly to the desired effect. Large mirrors should be laminated to sheets of plywood to guard against breakage.

Round mirrors, preferably concave, placed behind cabin lights as reflectors greatly increase the useful light from low wattage light bulbs and kerosene lamps.

Kerosene cabin lamps are desirable on sail boats, even though electric lights are installed. They should be all brass, mounted in full gimbals or in half gimbals so they remain level when the boat is heeled. A metal heat and smoke shield should be attached to the lamp installation some distance above the top of the glass chimney to protect the overhead. Chimneys should be removed while under way to prevent breakage, and spare chimneys should be carried. Lamp bowls should be kept three-quarters full, and daily filling may be required if lamps are used every evening. Wicks which burn with an uneven flame should be trimmed evenly, and several spare wicks should be aboard. Chimneys should be kept free of soot. When cool they may be washed in water with detergent, rinsed and dried. Pieces of newspaper are ideal for polishing lamp chimneys as the ink acts as a polishing agent. Do not immerse hot lamp chimneys in water since they are apt to break from thermal shock.

Curtains should be of a relatively open weave but of heavy cloth, similar to burlap or monk's cloth. They should be sufficiently full to provide complete privacy when drawn. Dark colors are best as they do not show dirt readily. Colors should be chosen with regard to the colors of upholstery, trim, carpets and accessories. Synthetic cloth such as nylon or Dacron will be most practical, since they are not subject to mildew damage and melt rather than burn in case of fire. Fiberglass curtains are easiest to keep clean, but must be secured along top and bottom so they will not swing about while under way. Fiberglass will rapidly chafe and wear out if not secured in place. Fiberglass is rot proof, and stains and dirt do not permeate the fibers.

Wash fiberglass curtains by sloshing them loosely in a mixture of water and detergent, rinse in clean water and allow to drip dry. Do not wring since this will damage the fibers. Fiberglass curtains dry rapidly and can be rehung while still damp. Curtains made of other than glass cloth should be washed in water with detergent, rinsed and excess water squeezed out. A permanent-press fabric will dry smooth and not require ironing.

The cabin sole in most boats contains hatches or loose boards which can be removed to allow access to the bilges. Vinyl tile or seamless vinyl floor covering is often used to cover the cabin sole. Vinyl is clammy when barefooted and tends to be slippery, even when a textured surface is used. It must be kept waxed to protect the surface, and any good quality floor wax may be used. Sand must be kept off vinyl floor covering because, being sharp and abrasive, it will scratch the surface. Vinyl is easy to keep clean and stains will not penetrate a properly waxed surface. Because floor space is so limited, a whisk broom, or a child's broom on larger craft, and a plastic dust pan will be all that is needed for day-to-day housekeeping.

Fluffy nylon throw rugs may be strategically placed for comfort underfoot on a vinyl covered or wood sole. Small rugs must have a rubberized, nonskid backing to prevent accidental falls. Rugs should be taken on deck and shaken daily to remove sand and lint.

Indoor-outdoor carpet of Olefin fiber is widely used on boats today. It is waterproof, stains do not penetrate, it is not subject to mildew or rot and is readily washable without shrinking or fading. It is comfortable underfoot but feels somewhat harsher than wool or nylon carpeting. It will not ravel when cut and does not need bound or sewn edges. It can be laid loose or can be semi-permanently installed using liquid adhesive or double-faced adhesive tape. It cuts readily with a knife or scissors and is easy to install.

Olefin fiber carpet should be laid loosely without tape or adhesive so it can easily be taken on deck for cleaning. It lies flat even when installed loose. If desirable, cutouts can be made with a sharp knife around removable floorboards or hatches leading into the bilges so the carpet does not need to be lifted for access to the bilge.

Spills should be wiped up as they occur. Spots can be easily removed by scrubbing in place, using a stiff bristled brush, water and detergent. Sand and loose dirt can be readily removed from these carpets by taking them on deck and shaking them well. Should they appear dirty they can be spread out on deck or the pier and be scrubbed with a broom or brush, detergent and fresh water. Hang carpets on railings or lifelines and allow to drip dry. Since the fibers do not absorb water, the rug will dry completely in a very short time.

Olefin fiber carpeting is available in many colors and patterns in rolls of various widths in three-foot increments. Select a color and pattern which blends well with the color scheme used, preferably dark rather than light. It is sold by the running foot in each width roll. Measure the maximum length and width of the space you wish to cover on the cabin sole. If the width is three feet or less, purchase carpet from a roll three feet wide (if available) and in a length slightly longer than the maximum length to be covered. If the width of the space exceeds three feet or if three-feet-wide rolls of carpet are not available, purchase a length of carpet slightly longer than the width to be covered from a carpet roll whose width slightly exceeds the length of the space to be covered. This allows for the lowest cost with the least waste.

Lay the carpet in place on the cabin sole and, with a sharp knife or scissors, trim to fit the available space exactly. If you hesitate to work in this manner, make a paper pattern of the space to be covered (use brown wrapping paper) and trim the carpet before installation. Cutouts for access to the bilges can be made from the pattern or after the trimmed carpet is installed.

Soft, nylon throw rugs in contrasting or complementing colors can be used on top of Olefin carpets beside berths for added comfort when barefooted, and to serve as color accents. A similar rug in the head will be appreciated and can be removed for cleaning.

Leftover scraps remaining from installation of your Olefin fiber carpet can be glued to steps of the companionway ladder to provide a skid proof surface. Cockpit seats can also be covered with indoor-outdoor carpet taped or glued in place. However, when used in this manner on flat, outdoor surfaces, the carpeting will hold spray and rainwater for quite awhile, so cockpit cushions must be used to provide dry seating when the cockpit carpeting is damp.

Sharp edges of lockers, cabinets and partial bulkheads can also be padded in an attractive, nautical manner by using large diameter twisted line held in place by brads or wire nails and edged with cove or quarter round molding, as illustrated in Figure 14.

Strips of this carpeting can be used as padding and glued to carlins, beams, locker edges and tops, etc. It should be edged with wood molding when used to pad vertical corners to prevent its being loosened.

Olefin fiber carpeting is also available in one-foot squares with adhesive, double-sided tape applied to one side. These carpet squares, or an equivalent strip of carpeting, can be applied to the inner surface of the hull

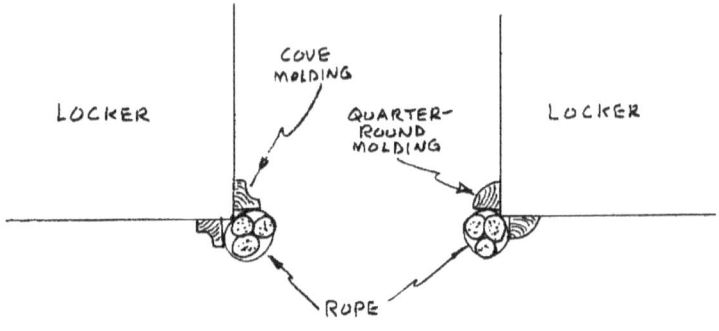

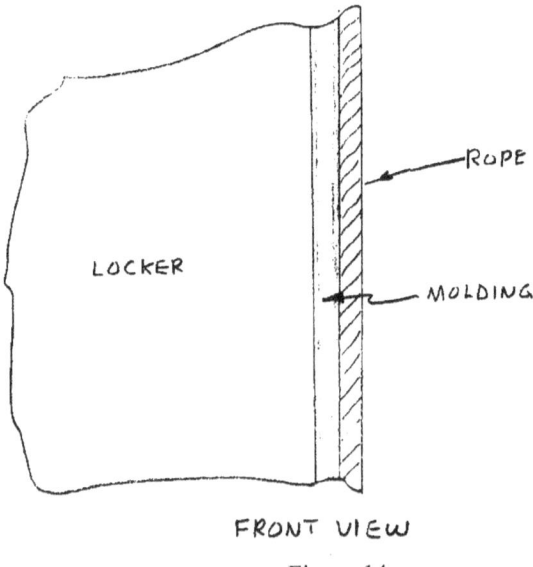

Figure 14

Edge Padding With Rope.

along the outboard side of each berth where no ceiling is present. This prevents condensation from dampening bedding and provides padding which makes the lee berth much more comfortable. This is particularly applicable to fiberglass boats, especially in the forward cabin which is equipped with vee-berths. It also contributes to the cozy feeling which should be in every boat cabin.

Berth mattresses and the seats of settee berths, convertible dinettes, etc., should be polyurethane foam three inches or more thick. Five-inch thick foam makes an extremely comfortable mattress. Back rests can be as thin as two inches, but thicker ones will be more comfortable. All cushions, back rests and mattresses should be removable for airing and for cleanliness. Coverings may be of vinyl or nylon or other synthetic fabric, and should be stain resistant and easy to keep clean with detergent and water, or upholstery shampoo.

Polyurethane foam is sanitary, odorless, waterproof, rot proof and does not mildew. It is extremely long lasting and can take hard use without breaking down, compressing or crumbling. It is far better than other materials formerly used, including foam rubber, cotton, kapok and rubberized hair. When used on boats, protected by synthetic or plastic covers, it requires no care except keeping the covering clean and occasional exposure to the sun to prevent musty odors.

Leecloths should be installed on all berths. Permanent leeboards make the berth somewhat uncomfortable to use as a seat, but keep mattresses and cushions in place and help the sleeper remain in his bunk on the weather side. If the boat is subject to much heel (this includes all sail boats) it is simple to provide comfortable leecloths of canvas which keep the weather berth occupant in place no matter what the motions of the boat.

A strip of eight or ten ounce canvas four feet long and 18 inches wide, is required for each berth. One four-foot edge is fastened along the inboard edge of the berth with copper tacks or oval-headed screws and finish washers. Brass grommets are sewn into the two free corners, which should be reinforced with a double thickness of cloth, as shown in Figure 8. A pair of screw eyes are installed in the overhead, directly above the inboard edge of the berth and the same distance apart as the grommets. Small diameter nylon lines are secured to each grommet and their running ends spliced to pelican hooks or spring snap hooks. In use, the canvas leeboard is extended upwards and the lines secured to the screw eyes in the overhead. When not in use it can be stowed neatly beneath the berth mattress.

Medical and first aid supplies deserve a location of their own where they will be handy but out of the way of any children aboard. Make up your own kit or purchase one made especially for boat use. Ready-made kits available in drug and auto supply stores are inadequate since they are designed for different circumstances. As a minimum you should have adhesive bandages, gauze in pads and rolls, adhesive tape, scissors, thermometer, an effective antiseptic, fungicide, antibiotic ointment, burn ointment, aspirin, antacid tablets, and prescription drugs if you require them. A conference with your doctor, covering the plans for your trip and the possibility of illness or accident, will result in excellent guidance and any prescriptions necessary for you to purchase the items he recommends.

Medical supplies should be kept in a portable watertight container. A war surplus ammunition box is an excellent container and is very inexpensive. Paint it green with a white or red cross on top and all four sides. Such a portable container allows aid to be brought to the patient rather than vice versa, and will save many steps and eliminate delay when time may be important.

Every boat should have a library, even if it consists only of navigation texts and paperback detective stories. There is usually a lot of unoccupied time aboard, especially on a cruise, and nearly everyone enjoys reading. Book racks with lipped shelves and shock cord or sea rails to restrain the books should be a part of your decorating scheme. Separate bookcases can be secured to the bulkheads. Often there are shelves tucked up under the side decks which are ideal for books. Almost any unused space can be used to stow books.

The choice of books is such an individual thing that it is difficult to make intelligent suggestions. However, in addition to the navigational books, charts, and other publications normally on board, you'll need manufacturer's instruction manuals and leaflets for every piece of the boat's equipment. You may wish to add books about boating, cruising, seamanship, boat handling, weather forecasting, stories of voyages and the sea, and boating magazines, plus possibly guides to fish and sea shells, a cookbook or two, a good First Aid manual, travel guidebooks, foreign language phrase books and books relating to your work or your other hobbies. Fiction books, novels and short stories, may also be desired for light reading. Many excellent books are available in paperback editions. These take less space than hard cover editions, are light weight, and inexpensive. Except for books which you intend to keep for permanent reference and which you use often (including *this* book, of course!) you should concentrate on getting paperback editions of any book available.

Most shoreside houses have pictures on the wall, growing plants, and various knick-knacks and art objects scattered about accenting the overall decorating plan. This is not possible to the same degree on a boat, nor as desirable. Loose objects like ashtrays, table lighters, cigarette boxes, candlesticks, etc., must be stowed before getting underway. Pictures must be small, the subject matter suitable to the location, and frames securely fixed to bulkheads. Nautical paintings, lithographs and photographs can be used sparingly. Plants should be small, require little water, and be fixed securely so they cannot come unshipped and scatter dirt around in the cabin. They are really out of place on a boat, and impractical unless plenty of fresh water is available.

Useful as well as decorative are the nautical looking ship's clock and matching barometers in polished brass or chrome. These should be solidly mounted on the bulkhead in the cabin. They may be mounted near each other or flanking a door or even on opposite sides of the cabin. Their location should be selected with an eye to symmetry and the overall effect on the cabin's appearance. Keep the cases bright, shining, dust free. A tissue moistened in alcohol or a product similar to *Bon-Ami Dust n' Wax* should be used to polish chrome and lacquered brass. Uncoated brass requires metal polish, but after polishing it may be sprayed with two light coats of any clear liquid acrylic plastic. Be sure to mask the glass face and any openings in the case with paper and masking tape before spraying with plastic. Chrome plated cases should not be sprayed.

A rope mat makes for safe and handy, non-slip footing in the galley and cockpit. You can easily make your own from lines which are still essentially good but which have been retired from active service. Three-eighth inch diameter line is easiest to handle. The line should be Flemished down on a flat surface in a tight spiral of the desired diameter for the finished mat. Using nylon thread or cord (fishing line is excellent and inexpensive) and curved needle, sew adjacent turns of line together, following around the spiral from the center to the end, keeping the rope mat flat. When sewing is completed, turn the mat over. The unsewn side may be sewn to make a stronger mat but this is not necessary. The mat will provide secure footing and resists sliding, even on a smooth cockpit or cabin sole. When dirty, the mat should be scrubbed clean with a brush, detergent and water, rinsed well and hung in the rigging or over the lifeline to dry. It should be secured so it will not slip over the side and sink. Polyethylene line, which floats, can be used to make a mat but is slippery, and harsh underfoot. Twisted or braided nylon or Dacron make the best mats.

Spares and materials needed for repair which should be maintained depend primarily on the way in which your boat is used. If you spend most of your time in the marina and only go out occasionally for a daylight sail for a few hours, you need carry only those parts and materials necessary to allow you to jury-rig as necessary and get safely back to shore. A set of plugs and points and a few bits of assorted hardware will suffice in this instance, since most maintenance and repair will be done in the marina where you have ready access to the stocks of marine dealers and hardware stores.

At the other extreme is the blue water cruising boat crossing an ocean or sailing around the world. In this case, the spares situation becomes acute and everything necessary must be carried on board. There are no stores in the middle of the ocean, nor repairmen. All contingencies must be anticipated and spare parts and materials must be carried to cover practically every eventuality from a broken shear pin to a lost set of sails or a broken-down engine. As a general rule, replacement parts should be carried for everything that moves: Engine, head, stove, sails, rigging, pumps, blowers, etc. The particular varieties of items to carry are replacements for things that may break, wear out or be used up, and are suggested in the text of the various chapters of this book. Each skipper should make a check list of quantities of those of the following items which he feels should be aboard in case of need.

Engine spares (gaskets, plugs, points, condensers, injectors, fuel and water pump, needles.)
Stove (generator, hardware.)

Head (joker valve, pump parts, hardware, hose, fittings)

Paint (bottom, topside, boot-topping, interior, varnish.)   Tools (including brushes, sponges.)

Rigging (lines, wire, clamps, turnbuckles, hardware, blocks.)

Ground tackle (line, chain, shackles, swivels.)

Pumps (leathers, O-rings, impellers, hardware.)

Electrical (wire, switches, fuses, lamp bulbs, sockets.)

Sails (repair kit, spare sails, covers, awnings, dodgers.)   Hardware (hooks, cleats, fairleads, clamps, cotter pins/rings, screws, nuts, bolts, washers.)

Fuel (gasoline, motor oil, diesel fuel, kerosene, alcohol, bottled gas.)

Lighting (lamp chimneys and wicks, light bulbs, fuses)

Medical (drugs, bandage, antiseptic.)

Cleaning (detergent, wax, bronze or stainless steel wool, metal polish.)

Hull (wood plugs, plywood, fiberglass cloth, epoxy.)

Steering, running (shear pins, propeller, rudder, tiller.)

Stores (food, water, matches, toilet tissue, soap, spare generator, bronze wool scrubbers.)

Plumbing (tubing, fittings, hose, clamps, nipples, valves, seacocks, outlets.)

Miscellaneous (marline, thread, wire, tape, canvas, tacks, adhesive, bedding compound.)

Spare parts and materials should be carefully stowed and a chart made showing their locations in the boat so they may be found rapidly when needed. A notation should be made in the log when any spares are used so they may be replaced at the first opportunity.

Basic Boat Maintenance - - *J. Frank Brumbaugh*

CHAPTER SEVEN
INSTRUMENTS AND ELECTRONICS

Instruction manuals and pamphlets supplied by the instrument and equipment manufacturers are the best source of pertinent maintenance information for these expensive and relatively delicate items. These should be kept where they are readily available for reference. If any are missing, damaged, or misplaced, write to the manufacturer for a duplicate, giving the name, model and serial number (if any) of the equipment for which you are requesting an instruction manual.

All electrical repairs and internal adjustments should be made only by qualified electronic technicians. In the case of radio telephones and radar, the technician must possess a valid Radiotelephone License issued by the FCC (Federal Communications Commission). Radar repair requires the license carry a Radar endorsement. Amateur radio equipment can be adjusted and maintained by the owner of any FCC Amateur Operator's License of the same or higher class than the station equipment. The Amateur, or "ham" as he is called, is usually capable of maintaining all other electronic equipment (radio receivers, LORAN, GPS, depth sounder, television sets, etc.) which are not by law required to be serviced by a holder of an FCC Commercial Radiotelephone license.

All electronic equipment which is reasonably

heavy or which is connected to an external antenna (aerial) must be mounted securely so they cannot come unshipped accidentally. In general, this category includes radio telephones, LORAN receivers, radar, GPS, direction finders, amateur Radio equipment, and television sets. Most depth sounders, fuel vapor detectors, and communications receivers are also securely mounted. Only small, portable equipment such as loud hailers and radios which are used in different places above and below decks are not secured in place.

Shock mountings are used for some equipment while others are mounted directly to the structure. Use whichever type mounting was supplied with the equipment. Do not attempt to design your own shock mounts for electronic equipment. It is far more difficult than bolting rubber mounted supports to the equipment and the mathematics involved in the design of shock mountings are formidable. For the same reason, do not use a shock mount on one piece of equipment intended for another, even if it seems to fit. The results may, under vibration and shock while under way, damage the equipment permanently.

In general, keep all electronic equipment free of dust. A very light coating of wax on smooth painted surfaces or a light coating of oil on crackle finished surfaces is recommended. Dirt which accumulates on panels around much-used knobs and switches should be removed with a soft cloth dampened with detergent in water. Dial windows should be cleaned with a tissue dampened in alcohol or any commercial glass cleaner. All connections of wires and cables should be kept tight. Mounting hardware and screws holding dust covers and covers of access ports should be tight.

Knobs must be tight and pointers must be correctly oriented. Knobs may have one or two set-screws and must be maintained tight. If a knob becomes loose or comes off, tighten set-screws temporarily and turn as far to the left (counterclockwise) as it will go without using excess force. If the pointer or index line does not point directly at the farthest left calibration mark on the panel, loosen the set-screw. Set the knob so the index or pointer is at the farthest left calibration mark on the panel. Tighten set-screws permanently.

Replacement of the picture tube in a television set, while simple, should not be attempted except by someone who knows what he is doing. Accidental breakage of a picture tube causes shards of glass, some of which are coated with a poisonous fluorescent powder, to fly about with explosive force, much as a hand grenade or small bomb loaded with broken glass shrapnel. The large picture tube is evacuated and contains a vacuum, resulting in enormous pressures exerted on the outer surface, pressures exceeding 24,190 pounds per square foot -- over 12 tons. When the tube is broken, air rushes into the vacuum to relieve this pressure. This is technically called an implosion, but the results are very similar to an explosion where the same forces are involved.

There are three different types of depth sounders available, all of which operate on the same principles but present depth information differently. All require a transducer to be mounted beneath the water surface with its active face directed towards the bottom. The face of the transducer must never be painted. It should be kept free of marine growth and will only operate with the transducer submerged properly in water.

One type of depth sounder gives the depth of water in Arabic numerals in liquid crystal (LCD) or light-emitting diode (LED) displays. These depth sounders accurately give the depth of the water but no other information. Remember that depth sounders of every kind always indicate the depth of water between the face of the transducer and the bottom. If the keel extends below the transducer -- and it does in most installations -- mentally subtract the vertical distance from the bottom of the keel and the face of the transducer to determine the actual depth of water beneath the keel. some models can be calibrated for the depth to the keel.

The remaining type of depth sounder draws a profile of the bottom on a small screen, similar to a video display. A hard bottom is indicated by a thin, sharp bottom line. A broader, softer line indicates a soft bottom. Fish are indicated by spots between the bottom and the surface. This is the most expensive depth sounder, and finds its main use on boats used primarily for fishing.

Any depth sounder will provide accurate depth measurements beneath a boat at rest or moving slowly through the water. Few will operate while traveling at high speeds because the water becomes turbulent and often filled with air bubbles around the transducer. Too, the vast majority of depth sounders available and practical for use aboard boats indicate the water depth directly below the boat. They will not warn of approaching banks, large rocks, etc., ahead of the boat. Used intelligently, however, they replace the hand lead line and provide continuing water-depth information.

Transducers are generally mounted through the hull with a fairing block between the hull and the body of the transducer. This is required on all but fiberglass boats which have solid hulls. If the hull contains honeycomb, as many modern hulls are constructed, the air spaces between inner and outer plastic skins of the hull preclude internal mounting of the transducer, and it will have to be through-hull mounted. Fiberglass hull materials are essentially transparent to ultrasonic impulses, merely attenuating the strength of the signal somewhat. This can be compensated for by a slight increase in gain (by twisting the gain control clockwise -- to the right). The transducer can be mounted inside the solid hull of a fiberglass boat.

Every vessel which sails out of sight of land, especially one crossing an ocean, must have either a competent navigator aboard along with his expensive sextant and *Nautical Almanac* and other navigation tools or, as is far more common today, a simple GPS (Global Position Receiver). These small handheld receivers accept signals from at least two but preferably three or more of the many orbiting satellites in the GPS system, and show position in latitude and longitude within 100 to 300 feet, no matter where one is in the world on land or sea or in an aircraft. Cost for a GPS starts at about $150, depending upon the many other features available on some models. It takes but a few minutes to learn how to use the GPS receiver. No offshore boat should ever be without one.

New rulings of the FCC require the first radiotelephone installed on a pleasure boat be operable in the VHF-FM (very high frequency-frequency modulation) band. There are several channels available, static is practically nonexistent and congestion is much less. These advantages are gained at the expense of higher initial cost and greatly reduced operating range. 25-watt VHF-FM radiotelephone sets, the maximum power allowed by law, cost $150.00 or more. The maximum distance over which two stations can communicate rarely exceeds 50 miles, and usually is in the vicinity of 25 miles. Only a short antenna is used, and no radio ground plate is needed. (One should be installed as a part of the grounding and lightning protection system even though it is not specifically required for proper operation of VHF-FM radiotelephones.)

Single side-band, or SSB, radiotelephones operating in the short wave marine bands may not be installed and licensed unless there is an existing, licensed VHF-FM radiotelephone installed on your boat. This is not necessarily a hardship for the VHF-FM set will meet all your needs on inland waters and close to shore. SSB is used to cover greater distances, up to 6000 miles or more, depending on frequency. The maximum power allowed for SSB is 150 watts and such an installation will cost over $3,000.00. Lower powered sets will cost somewhat less, but none could be considered inexpensive.

Radio telephones, both VHF-FM and SSB, allow boats so equipped to contact the Coast Guard, other boats, and to call any telephone in the world through Marine Operators ashore. The installation, tuning and servicing of all but specific Install-it-yourself, pretuned radiotelephones, whether VHF-FM or SSB, can only be done legally by a qualified technician who is a holder of the proper type and grade of FCC license.

Radar is a valuable piloting aid and provides a bird's-eye view of the area around the boat, showing the coast line, other boats and some buoys and other aids to navigation. It can be installed, tuned and serviced legally only by a licensed technician who holds an FCC license with a radar endorsement.

LORAN is a passive system of position finding which requires a specialized but fairly inexpensive radio receiver. It contains a small LCD screen displaying position and other navigation data. Operation is a simple process and can be learned by anyone within a short time. LORAN enables determination of your boat's position at sea at any time of day or night, within minutes, in those areas of the oceans covered by LORAN transmissions from shore stations. Accuracy is usually within 50- to 150-feet at worst. LORAN is as simple to install as a television set -- hook it up to a power source and connect an antenna -- and a licensed technician is not required for servicing. However, LORAN should only be serviced by a technician familiar with marine electronics in general and LORAN in particular because of its electronic complexity. Don't take your LORAN receiver to your friendly neighborhood radio-television repairman; you may regret it. LORAN has been superseded by GPS on most vessels.

Global Positioning System (GPS) receivers are superficially similar to LORAN in that they display, either on LCD or video screens, position, course, speed, etc. anywhere in the world on land, sea, or in the air. A series of orbiting satellites transmit time and position signals which are picked up by the small antennas on GPS receivers. The receiver locks onto three or more satellites which are above the horizon and converts the received signals to the position of the boat, usually in longitude and latitude, course since last plot, speed over ground, course to steer, etc. The GPS receiver updates its displayed information each second. A GPS can be programmed with waypoints and will warn as each is approached, indicating course and time to the next waypoint.

GPS is not expensive, ranging in price from a low of about $150 to a high of several hundred dollars. However, because this system provides coverage over the entire surface of the earth, it is always ready for use. LORAN, on the other hand, is available only near shore and was never intended to be global in coverage. Anyone sailing beyond US waters should invest in a GPS rather than LORAN.

The fastest acting, most accurate GPS receivers, which give position within 100 to 300 feet, will receive three or more separate channels and cost very close to the minimum, which is a discounted price available through several marine discount companies. Disregard claims of the number of satellites the GPS will receive. Check instead it has three or more channels. Three separate channels, processing data from three satellites, are all that are required to plot an accurate position on the surface.

Each satellite transmits its information during a 20 millisecond (0.02 second) burst. A GPS with *fewer* than three channels must use multiplexing, sampling the data from three or more satellites but cannot listen to any single satellite for the 20 milliseconds. This is why, for best position accuracy, a GPS receiver should have at least three channels. More channels increase accuracy -- four satellites are needed to establish position and altitude of aircraft -- but unless more than three channels are actually needed, the cost will be far greater than the value of the slight increase in accuracy of position.

Radios and television sets on the boat require the same care and may be serviced the same as those ashore. Radios have much value as entertainment as well as sources of news and weather broadcasts. Radios can also be used as direction finders in a pinch. Television receivers are usable only within 100 miles or so offshore, unless you subscribe to satellite TV. However, this is not practical because normal motion of the boat precludes aiming the small dish antenna at the satellite.

The compass is the most important navigational instrument on your boat after your GPS receiver. It must be installed so its lubber line is on or parallel to the fore-and-aft line of the boat. It should be mounted as far as practical from the engine or other large mass of ferrous metal (iron or steel). Keep steel tools, exposure meters, radios, beer and soft drink cans, and other metals away from the compass. Even a pocket knife, nail clip or key ring in your pocket can deflect the compass if you stand close to it. So can a steel belt buckle. Make a deviation table for the compass with rigging and normal stores in their usual locations.

Basic Boat Maintenance - - *J. Frank Brumbaugh*

Magnetic compasses are quite simple mechanically and will often outlast the boat. Liquid-filled compasses should be kept full so no large bubble is present above the card since this can cause errors by introducing friction. Use only the fluid specified by the compass manufacturer when fluid is added.

Sextants, binoculars, cameras, chronometers, stopwatches, and clocks should be periodically checked by a qualified instrument repairman and adjusted or repaired as required. This is especially important if such instruments have been dropped.

Your barometer can be most useful in forecasting the local weather if you learn how to use it. The barometer should be mounted permanently inside the cabin. When first installed, and periodically thereafter, it should be adjusted to the correct sea level reading. A phone call to the local Coast Guard station or National Weather Service Office will give you the barometer reading corrected to sea level -- approximately 30 inches. On the rear (occasionally on the front) of the barometer is a small adjusting screw accessible through a hole in the case. Use a small screwdriver to turn this screw *slightly* in the direction the barometer needle must move to show the correct pressure while gently tapping the barometer face with your finger and watching the needle. Continue to adjust this screw and tap the barometer until your barometer reading is the same as that of the Coast Guard or Weather Station. Occasional readjustment may be necessary for absolute accuracy, but is not of great importance since it is the *direction* of pressure change and the *speed* with which it changes which serves to indicate weather changes, not the actual barometer reading at any particular time. Barometers rarely require servicing, and if dropped and broken, they should be replaced rather than repaired. For a simple, easy-to-understand system for forecasting your local weather at sea for from 6 to 48 hours ahead, refer to *Marine Weather Forecasting*, by J. Frank Brumbaugh, Bristol Fashion Publications.

Engine instruments and electrical meters occasionally have their glass faces broken. Remove the instrument and have the glass replaced by an instrument repairman. Compare the cost of repair to that of replacement. Some instruments are better replaced than repaired. As a rule of thumb, if the instrument looks expensive, is well made, with a smooth case held together by bright screws, it will probably pay to have it repaired. Conversely, if it looks cheap and roughly made and the case is die-formed and held on by bent tabs of metal, replace it rather than having it repaired.

CHAPTER EIGHT
BILGE WATER AND LEAKS

A little water in the bilges may be completely normal or may warn of impending trouble. A lot of water in the bilge indicates neglect or major problems which require immediate investigation. Water entering from an unknown source, or in larger quantities than normal from a known source, should be looked into. Once you learn where the water is coming from you either know you have nothing to worry about or you know what you have to do to halt it. Not knowing can be dangerous!

A boat floats on -- or in -- water, and it is natural to want to keep the water outside the boat where it belongs. Some water will accidentally get below through hatches and ventilators. Water in the bilges of wooden boats is quite normal, as are small amounts in boats with inboard engines. All areas within the bilges should be accessible and ventilated, or at least sufficiently open so that normal air flow reaches all surfaces and there are no dead air pockets. This is especially important in wood boats and in boats equipped with inboard or inboard/outboard engines. Seepage occurs in wood boats through even well-caulked seams as the hull planks work. Water seeps through properly installed shaft logs where it provides lubrication and cooling for the engine shaft. Occasional pumping will remove this normal seepage.

Every boat should be equipped with at least one high capacity manually operated bilge pump in addition to any electric pumps which may be aboard. Be sure the manpower available to man the pumps matches the pumps you have. A bilge pump with no one to operate it is worthless in an emergency. Small amounts of bilge water are easily handled by an electric bilge pump which turns on automatically as water reaches a predetermined level, turning itself off when the water level has been reduced to minimum by pumping. As long as the boat's batteries are up to charge, the pump motor wiring is intact and the fuse is not blown, the electric bilge pump will reliably keep the bilges reasonably dry unless a bad leak or other source of water brings water in more rapidly than the limited capacity of the pump to remove.

Intake hoses to bilge pumps should be screened to prevent debris from entering the pump where it could cause damage or stoppage. Hoses should lead from the lowest point in the bilges so practically all bilge water will be removed by the pump. Make certain your hoses are of the proper construction and type so they will not collapse under suction. A collapsed hose renders a bilge pump worthless and can cause the motor of an electric pump to burn out. Limber holes must be kept open -- clear them with a length of stiff wire -- and all debris and trash should be kept out of the bilges. Paper is particularly bad in wet bilges since it will clog limber holes, hose screens and strainers. Labels from canned foods may become loosened due to dampness and drop into the bilges. Sawdust, chips, shavings, plastic and other debris must be kept out of the bilges.

The bilges of wood boats should have all exposed wood surfaces treated with a good wood preservative or paint. Oily surfaces should be cleaned and the bilges kept free from oil. A particularly dirty bilge can be cleaned by emptying a box of detergent into the bilges, adding water and taking the boat out for an hour or two to slosh the detergent and water around thoroughly. The bilges should then be pumped dry, rinsed with clear water and pumped dry again. It is against the law to flush bilges in harbors or marinas, and is punishable by fine or imprisonment. It is also discourteous to other boat owners whose topside may be stained by the oil and other substances pumped from your bilges. Rock salt strewn in the bilges of wood boats -- particularly those kept in fresh water -- will prevent rot from forming. Use plenty of salt; it's cheap insurance.

Merely cleaning an oily or greasy bilge is not sufficient; the source of oil must be determined. Oil slicks on bilge water can be caused by petroleum lubricant in the shaft housing of inboard engines. This is normal and the amount of oil is minimal, making a thin oil slick. Slicks which are heavy or which indicate leakage of gasoline or diesel fuel require the source be located and the leak repaired. Engine maintenance is discussed in Chapter Nine.

In some boats the ice box is allowed to drain into the bilge. This water often contains bits of food and is a source of odors in any boat. In wood boats it promotes rot. This problem is discussed in Chapter Five. Even if you have to install a drip pan or pump, arrange for the ice box to drain over the side. Don't use your bilges for a sewer.

The probable source of excess bilge water in a boat kept in salt water can often be determined by the simple expedient of tasting the bilge water. If this method sounds unattractive, perhaps your bilges need a thorough cleaning.

If the taste is strongly salt, the probable sources include the shaft log, loose through-hull fittings, hull leaks, leaky hoses on underwater seacocks, or spray taken aboard.

A fresh or slightly brackish taste indicates deck leaks, rain coming through ventilators or hatches, leaks in fresh water tanks, plumbing lines or drains, etc.

While the taste test is only effective on salt water it does eliminate a number of possibilities and makes the search for the source of the excessive water somewhat easier. Tanks, plumbing lines, seacocks, hoses and drains are discussed in Chapter Five. These should be thoroughly checked whenever fresh water in the bilges cannot be attributed to rain water coming below.

Rain water generally finds its way below through leaky decks, ventilators, or windows, ports and hatches inadvertently left open. Deck leaks are relatively common on older, wood boats. Caulking or covering (usually with fiberglass) is the only solution.

Leaks often occur around hatch coamings, where the trunk cabin or deck house sides meet the deck, around masts stepped on the keel, around pipes, ventilators or fittings passing through decks and cabin tops. Proper fitting and fastening of joints and the use of waterproof glue, epoxy cements, bedding compound, caulking, etc., will stop leaks at the source.

Leaks overhead are a common source of discomfort below. It seems most such leaks make themselves known by dripping on a berth and its harried occupant. Rarely is the source of the leak at the point where the water is dripping. Usually it is some distance away. These leaks may be difficult to trace to their source as the longitudinal path of the water may be partly hidden behind ceiling or inside a paneled overhead. Water always runs down hill, so direct your search to levels somewhat higher above the waterline than the drip. Leaks must be stopped at the source. At sea, minor leaks in the decks and superstructure can often be temporarily repaired by a deft application of caulking or bedding compound.

Ventilators should be constructed on the Dorade principle if they are expected to do their job properly without conducting water below. Rain and spray which enter ventilator inductors should be separated from the air stream and allowed to drain. This is easily accomplished, as a glance at cutaway views of several types of ventilators illustrated in Figure 15 will indicate. Baffles and/or lips on the air conduit leading below prevents water from entering. Water which enters the ventilator is prevented from getting below since it is shunted from the air stream by the baffle or lip and drains from the base of the ventilator through small holes or slots which serve as scuppers.

Rotating, wind-driven exhaust ventilators prevent water from entering by the design of the vanes on the rotating head. As it spins it not only sucks air from the interior of the boat, thus tending to blow water away from the slots between vent vanes, but the centrifugal force generated by rotation also tends to throw the water out. While not a particularly attractive nor nautical appearing ventilator, it is one of the most effective. Even a slight breeze will cause the head to rotate, exhausting stale air and drawing fresh air in through all ports and hatches which are open.

Fans and blowers are often used in the air stream of ventilators, usually to exhaust air, as in bilge and engine compartment ventilating systems. Powered ventilators should not depend on electric power for adequate ventilation, and should be capable of conducting air into and from the spaces in which they are installed, even if fan or blower motors become inoperative. Fan blades and squirrel cages should not obstruct normal air flow when power is off. Blades and vanes must be kept free of dust, and bearings should be lubricated as the manufacturer directs. Wiring and connections must be tight and in good condition. The proper operation of power blowers in ventilation of compartments in which volatile gasses from fuel or other sources may accumulate is of utmost importance to the safety of the boat. Only sealed spark-proof electric motors should be used where an explosive atmosphere may exist. Never connect or disconnect motors in such locations unless the Master electrical switch is open or off, removing power from all circuits except the bilge pump and alarm system.

    Repair of steel or aluminum hulls is beyond the ability of most boat owners and properly should be relegated to a qualified boatyard. Aluminum hull plates occasionally open at the welds, or may be split by contact with sharp, underwater obstructions. Most such damage will not allow more water to enter than can be handled by the pumps if the boat is properly equipped. Seams in steel hulls are subject to similar damage with comparable results.

    Caulking may come out of seams between planks in wood hulls, or either rot or a collision could causes a plank to break or split. A poor job of caulking, which should be done only by an expert, often results in seams opening when the boat is working in a seaway. Rot may cause a plank or rib to let go or collapse, and this always results from neglect in maintenance and repair. A minor collision which would not affect a sound hull can sink a boat with rot in her planks and frames.

    Fiberglass hulls are not nearly as subject to leaks as hulls of other materials. They have no seams to caulk, will not rot, is flexible and very strong. They can be cut or holed by sharp objects, however. Resulting holes are usually small and cuts or breaks quite narrow. Usually the pumps will take care of the excess water coming in through such leaks.

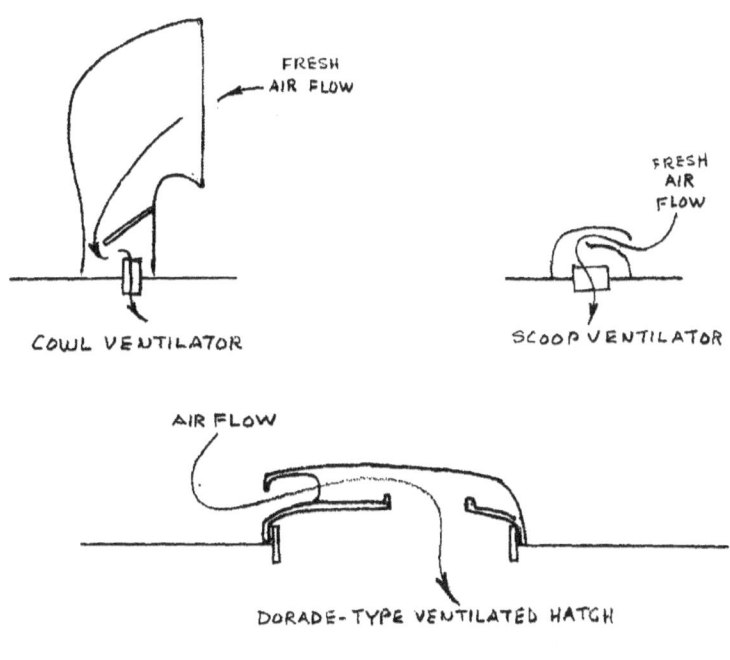

Figure 15

Ventilators.

The materials and workmanship used to effect major repairs, especially hull damage, should be equal to that used in original construction of your boat. Make personally sure of this important point. Do not leave it to the discretion and judgment of the boatyard doing the work.

The best method to plug an underwater leak (if it is small) is to drive a softwood plug firmly into the hole. Larger leaks should be stopped temporarily with such items as canvas, cushions, mattresses, plywood, planks, anything which can be jammed into or secured over the hole to halt or slow down the amount of water being taken on board. Materials used to plug large leaks should be applied from outside the hull if at all possible since water pressure will aid in keeping the plug in place. Passing lines under the boat to move the plug into place and hold it there can be done either by swimming the lines under the boat or by weighting the center of a bight of line and running it under the boat or running the boat over it. A SCUBA diver over the side can be of considerable help in placing the plug over the leak or jamming soft material into the leak from the outside. The diver must have a safety line tied between his waist and the boat so he can be pulled to the surface quickly in case of difficulty.

If it is impossible to reach and plug the leak from outside the hull, a reasonably good temporary patch can be applied from inside. Expose the inner surface of the hull where the leak is located, even if it is necessary to damage built-in furniture, ceiling or floorboards. Jam soft material -- clothing, towels, sheets, pillows, cushions, mattress, etc. -- into and over the leak. Cover them with plywood or planks (the floorboards or a locker door can be used) to keep them in place. Use lengths of wood, the boathook, whisker pole, swab or broom handle, anything available, to jam the cover over the leak so it remains in place. Brace the ends of these items against bulkheads, frames, wherever they will hold. Nails can be used in wood boats but no fastenings are possible with other hull materials.

Bulkheads which abut flooded compartments and hull sections adjacent to holed or weakened portions of the hull should be shored with whatever is available for dunnage. The bulkheads in pleasure boats are not designed to sustain the pressure of flooded compartments without being shored up.

Temporary repairs such as described above will usually reduce the water coming aboard to a volume which can be handled by the pumps, keeping your boat from sinking and allowing you to return to safety ashore. Go slowly through the water once you have patched the leak. Don't attempt to go as fast as your engine may drive you or the friction between the water and the patch may dislodge it and cause you to founder and sink. Going slowly will get you safely ashore fastest; going fast can put your boat on the bottom and leave you floating in a life jacket wondering what you did wrong. "Slow and easy" should be the byword when you have suffered major hull damage.

It will be best to check with the boat manufacturer to determine how much flooding your boat can handle without foundering. This will prevent premature and unnecessary abandonment, and will also make orderly and timely abandonment possible should this become necessary. In general, if your boat still floats on a reasonably even keel, can be maneuvered, and your pumps keep the water level inside the hull from rising, even if insufficient to lower it, you should be able to save the boat. Make for shore or shallow water and keep the pumps manned.

While steel and aluminum hulls almost always require repairs be made by a qualified yard, and wood hulls should be repaired by the yard, it is possible for a good carpenter to repair a wood hull. He can replace frames and planks, add sister ribs and butt blocks, and refinish gouges. It is beyond the scope of this book to detail these repairs. A good carpenter will not need such general information and others should not attempt such repairs.

Fiberglass hull repair is fully within the capability of most boat owners and requires little skill. The materials necessary -- fiberglass tape, cloth and mat, epoxy and brushes -- are available at most marine supply dealers and ship's chandlers. The procedure is simple and easy, and if repairs are properly made the hull will be as strong or stronger than when the boat was new. See Figure 16.

Remove all damaged fiberglass around the hole. Tin snips or a hacksaw blade will do the job adequately. Then with a rasp, grinder or coarse file, bevel the edges of the hole from the outside as shown. Make this bevel shallow and extend it well back from the edges of the hole. Sand it smooth and remove the dust resulting from sanding. The hole is now ready for repair.

Cover a piece of heavy cardboard, *Masonite* or plywood with waxpaper and place it tightly against the inside of the hull so it covers the hole. Cardboard can be held in place with masking tape. Other materials should be braced in place.

Cut a piece of fiberglass mat the size and shape of the hole. Center it in the hole from the outside and apply epoxy to hold it in place.

Alternate glass cloth and mat, or use all cloth pieces, cutting each slightly larger than the one preceding, and epoxy them in place. The final layer should be cloth and should be slightly larger than the beveled area.

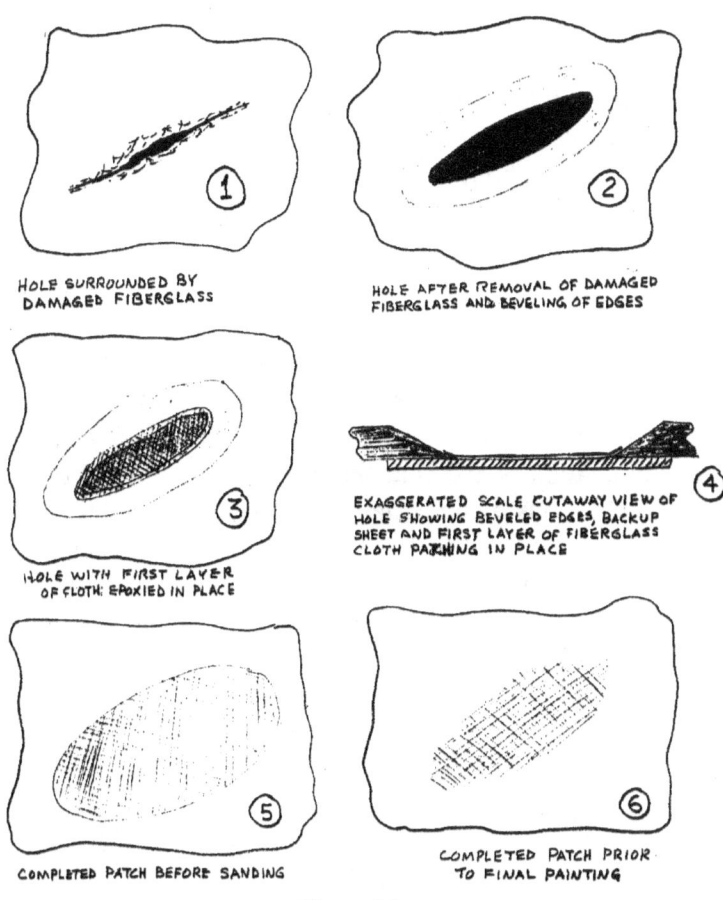

Figure 16

Patching Holes in Fiberglass Hulls

When the patch is complete, allow the epoxy to cure for 48 hours. Sand the patch smoothly, paying particular attention to feather the edges into the hull contour. Remove the dust resulting from sanding and paint over the patch to match the hull color. Antifouling paint must be applied to all patched areas below the waterline before the boat is returned to the water.

To complete the repair, remove the waxed

backing from the patch inside the hull. Remove all traces of wax and oil. Cut a piece of fiberglass cloth an inch or two larger than the patched area. Apply inside the hull over the patch with epoxy and allow it to cure. The patched area should now be as sound as the hull. The interior surface of the patch may be left bare or painted as desired.

If your boat has been removed from the water to effect repairs or for any other purpose, always check that all seacocks, shaft logs and through-hull fittings are secure and in place before returning the boat to the water. This should be done even if a competent boatyard has made the repairs. No boat should ever be launched unless the skipper has made certain all is well, especially below the waterline. After launching, carefully inspect the bilges and all plumbing and through-hull fittings to make certain there are no leaks or damage.

CHAPTER NINE
ENGINES

The boat's engines, inboard or outboard, supply motive power and in some instances charge the batteries, provide electricity, pump water, etc. This chapter is concerned with gasoline and diesel engines used for any purpose aboard pleasure boats. All engines, gasoline or diesel, must be carefully inspected before use when new and after each overhaul. Before starting the engine the following should be checked.

Gasoline Engine

Pre-operation Check

Check level of oil in crankcase (4-cycle only). Use oil viscosity recommended by manufacturer. This is usually SAE 5W20 or SAE 10W-30 for operation where temperatures fall below zero, and SAE 10W-30 or 20W-40 where high temperatures are expected.

Gear boxes not lubricated by the main engine lubrication system require lubricant added to the gear box. Follow manufacturer's recommendations.

Generator or alternator and starting motor bearings should be lubricated with light oil (SAE 10).

Fresh water cooling systems must have coolant added.

Check spark plugs are tightly in place and

ignition wires are connected in the proper firing order.

Check boat's batteries and connections. Batteries should be fully charged, electrolyte at the proper level and connections tight and not corroded.

Check fuel tanks. These should be full of gasoline of the proper octane rating for your engines. Fuel for 2-cycle engines must have oil added. Check manufacturer's instructions for grade of oil and recommended fuel to oil ratio (usually 100:1) although, most new engines over fifteen horsepower have a VRO system (Variable Ratio Oil).

Check gear shift to make certain it engages in forward and reverse and disengages in neutral.

Open all valves and seacocks in the sea water cooling system lines.

Add grease to dry fittings, if necessary. Check grease cups are full and tighten each a few turns. Grease cups may be located on water pump and shaft bearings.

Turn on blowers ventilating engine and fuel tank compartments. Check all tanks, fuel lines and connections for leaks. Open valves in fuel line to carburetor. Make sure flame arrestor on carburetor is in place.

Starting the Engine

Turn on ignition switch. Place gear shift in neutral position and open throttle slightly. Pull out choke knob. Press starting button.

Release starter button when engine starts, and set throttle for proper idling speed as indicated on tachometer.

Close choke slightly, gradually closing it completely as soon as engine will run on leaner mixture.

Check timing, particularly if engine runs roughly and adjust if necessary.

Check oil pressure. Refer to engine manufacturer's instructions.

Check water circulation by observing water spurting from wet exhaust. Dry exhaust tone will change and become softer and deeper when water circulates. It may be necessary to increase engine speed somewhat before the water pump will pick up its suction.

Check ammeter (for generator and some alternators) or voltmeter (for some alternators). Batteries should be charging slightly.

Allow engine to run for several minutes until water temperature gauge starts to rise.

Engine Operational Check

After engine has warmed up, cast off and go out for a short run.

Operate the engine at various speeds to be certain it is in excellent condition.

Observe water temperature and oil pressure and make certain these are within the limits specified by the manufacturer.

Check packing gland and shaft bearings for overheating.

Bring boat to her mooring or alongside and reduce throttle so engine will idle. Gear shift should be at neutral.

Allow engine to idle for five minutes, then switch ignition off and close throttle. Make sure ignition is locked.

Close fuel valve in line at tank, and at carburetor if two valves are used.

Close sea cock in cooling water intake line.

Observe packing gland at stern for excessive leakage. A few drops of water each minute is sufficient; more than five or six requires the packing nut be tightened slightly.

A new or just overhauled engine requires special care during its first hours of operation. Crankcase oil should be changed after the first 20 or 30 hours of operation (4-cycle engines only). Filters in oil and fuel lines should be cleaned or replaced at the same time.

The operation of transmission gears and gear shift should be checked at this time. There should be no indication of any slippage in the gears since this will cause rapid wear. Follow the manufacturer's instructions closely in adjusting transmission gears.

Check and adjust tappets if necessary so valves will open correctly. Timing should also be checked and adjusted if required.

The packing gland should be inspected for excess leakage and tightened if necessary. Do not overtighten or the shaft will overheat and either bind or destroy the packing and allow excess water to enter the bilges.

The flame arrestor, and air cleaner if used, should be removed and cleaned before being replaced. If the screen on the arrestor becomes clogged, clean it in gasoline with a stiff brush. Do this work on the dock or on deck, not in the engine compartment, and *DO NOT SMOKE!*

Release the coupling (unless it is a universal joint) between the engine shaft and propeller shaft to check alignment between shafts. Severe misalignment can be removed by a slight repositioning of the engine. Also check stern bearing and strut bearing for alignment.

Apply a small amount of petroleum jelly to the breaker cam inside the distributor. Use only a very small amount since it will melt and could run into the points and cause difficulty.

Crankcase oil should be changed every 50 hours of engine operation or as recommended by the manufacturer.

After 150 engine hours the oil filter should be cleaned or replaced. Check propeller shaft alignment. Check packing gland and heat exchangers.

Once each year, preferably at the beginning of the boating season, all moving parts of the engine and transmission should be inspected, adjusted, lubricated and, if necessary, overhauled.

Diesel Engines

Inspection procedures for diesel engines are basically similar to those just given for gasoline engines, except diesel engines do not have electrical ignition systems and fuel is fed through injectors instead of a carburetor.

Pre-operational Check

Check that fuel tanks are clean and filled with the correct grade of diesel fuel. Open all fuel line valves.

Fill crankcase with the proper weight of diesel lubricating oil (usually SAE 30).

Inspect oil sumps for clutch and reverse gears, and fill with the proper weight oil unless they are lubricated by the main engine lubrication system.

Fresh water cooling systems should be filled to within two inches of the top. Do not fill completely full since there must be an air cushion to allow for expansion of the water as the engine heats.

If fuel filters with top vents are installed, open vents and do not close until fuel starts to flow out through them. Filters which are mounted at a higher level than fuel tanks or which require priming (rarely found except on very old boats) must be filled with oil by hand before starting the engine.

Lubricate valve and injector mechanisms. Use plenty of oil. Replace injector cover.

Starting the Engine

Place the throttle to the starting or idle position.

Press starting button. If engine does not start within 30 seconds, release button. Wait three minutes before again pressing starting button.

When the engine starts, check oil pressure gauge. If the pressure is lower than the range recommended by the manufacturer, stop engine and check lubrication system for blockages or leaks.

After the engine starts, check the wet exhaust for water spurting out indicating cooling water is circulating.

After running about 10 minutes at idle, stop the engine. Check lubricating oil and add oil to the proper level or add as recommended by the manufacturer.

Operational Check

Restart the engine and cast off. Run at a slow engine RPM and watch water and oil temperature gauges. Temperatures should stabilize within the ranges specified by the engine manufacturer.

Operate the engine at various speeds within its normal operating range. The engine should run smoothly and without difficulty.

Return to the mooring or alongside and shift to neutral. Retard the throttle to idle position and allow the engine to idle for five minutes. Then stop the engine by tripping the stop control.

Close fuel and water valves.

The lubricating oil level should be checked. Fuel and water valves must be opened and the sea water strainer (if used) checked. Fresh water cooling systems should be checked for water level.

After 20 or 25 hours operation, inspect fuel and lubricating oil filters. Clean water and sediment.

After 50 to 200 hours (depending on the manufacturer's recommendation) the crankcase oil and filter should be changed.

After 100 hours the air intake silencers, blowers and blower screens in the intake should be cleaned. Lubricate starter motor and alternator or generator bearings.

After 150 hours the lube oil filter should be replaced. Check valve clearances. Inspect water pumps. Tighten engine hold-down fastenings. Check transmission alignment.

After 500 hours check injector balance and timing, valve clearances, and backlash in all gears. Remove injectors and inspect tips for burning and pitting, replacing each in the position from which it was removed. Change oil in gear sumps not serviced with lubricating oil. Clean fuel tanks if possible.

A good diesel engine, properly maintained and serviced, should last as long or longer than the boat in which it is installed. Pistons and cylinder liners should be inspected after about 2500 hours but will rarely need replacement before 3500 hours.

Trouble shooting of engines is presented in tabular form. Table 8 covers gasoline engines of all kinds and Table 9 covers diesel engines. The most common troubles are considered in these tables; symptoms are described, the probable cause indicated and the proper remedial action given. Engines are so reliable and simple that it is within the capability of anyone with only a slight amount of mechanical knowledge to keep them running and in good operating condition.

Basic Boat Maintenance - - J. Frank Brumbaugh

TABLE 8
TROUBLESHOOTING - GASOLINE ENGINES

TROUBLE	PROBABLE CAUSE	REMEDY
Will not start	Ignition off Loose wiring Master switch off Battery low	Check switch position. Check wiring. Check master switch position. Check batteries.
Will not start Low compression	Worn rings Gummy rings Valve seating	Check cylinders individually by hand in firing order to locate low compression cylinder. Remove spark plug and measure compression with gauge. If compression is lower than normal, remove gauge and pour one ounce of machine oil into the cylinder. Replace gauge and again check pressure after two minutes. If reading is still low, trouble is with rings. Worn rings must be replaced. Gummed up rings can be loosened with kerosene. If rings remain stuck, piston must be pulled and rings replaced. Valves can be reground or replaced.
	Head gasket leaks Studs leaky	Take up on head bolts. Mix detergent with cooling water and turn engine over with starter. Soap suds indicate head gasket must be replaced. Leaky studs can be sealed with joint compound.
	Washers missing from spark plugs Washers compressed	Tighten spark plugs. Remove plugs and replace with new washers if necessary.

Basic Boat Maintenance - - J. Frank Brumbaugh

TABLE 8
TROUBLESHOOTING - GASOLINE ENGINES

TROUBLE	PROBABLE CAUSE	REMEDY
Will not start Carburetor troubles	Flooding	Wait five minutes before trying to start. Close choke.
	Mixture too rich or too lean.	Adjust carburetor according to manufacturer's instructions.
	Float stuck or leaking	Turn off fuel supply. Remove carburetor bowl. Check float. Replace if necessary.
	Fuel line plugged Tank ourlet plugged	Check that valve in fuel line is open. Close valves and remove fuel line. Clear with stiff wire or compressed air. Replace line at tank. While blowing through line open valve at tank, then close. Air should pass into tank. Replace line.
	Water in fuel	Drain water from carburetor and fuel filter into cup and dump over the side. Do not drain into bilge. Check fuel in tank by drawing off about one quart and straining through chamois leather. Gasoline will pass through leaving water behind. If water is present in tanks, have them pumped out and refilled with pure unadulterated gasoline. Check that tank vents are protected from entry of rain and spray. Fit vents with leather or rubber flaps to prevent water entering.
Will not start Water in cylinder	Cracked block Cracked exhaust manifold	Block must be replaced if cracked. Cracking usually caused by freezing. Crack in exhaust manifold allows water to enter cylinder through exhaust valve.
	Submerged engine has been salvaged and installed	Engine must be taken apart and cleaned. Engines salvaged from salt water should never be used until having been completely overhauled.
Will not start Adulterated fuel	Impurities in gasoline	Strain gasoline. Purchase future supplies from different source.
	Air cleaner missing or dirty	Clean or replace air cleaner.
Will not start No fuel at carburetor	Tank empty or leaking Fuel line leaking	Inspect tank and fuel level. Check fuel line and connections for leaks. Tighten fittings. Replace any leaking components.

Basic Boat Maintenance - - J. Frank Brumbaugh

TABLE 8
TROUBLESHOOTING - GASOLINE ENGINES

TROUBLE	PROBABLE CAUSE	REMEDY
Will not start Starter motor will not spin engine	Connections to starter motor or battery loose Solenoid defective Starter motor defective	Check electrical connections. Tighten or replace electrical fittings. Replace solenoid or starter motor if defective.
	Piston frozen in cylinder	Remove spark plug and pour in two ounces kerosene. If this does not loosen piston engine must be taken apart and overhauled. Piston seizure is caused either by lack of lubricating oil, lack of water in the water jacket or rust caused by long periods of idleness. The water jacket should be flushed out with hot water under pressure to remove rust, scale and salt deposits. Check water pump to see it is circulating water.
Will not start Crank shaft, rod or wrist pin bent or broken	Lack of lubrication Propeller shaft seized	Check crankcase oil level. Inspect shaft bearings and clear seizure. Lubricate, dismantle engine and repair.
Will not start Starting gear frozen	Bendix gear	Rock flywheel by hand with ignition off and transmission in neutral to release starter gear. Remove starter and check spring on drive pinion. Replace if weak or broken. Bendix gear should slide freely on shaft. Oil if necessary. Clean teeth on flywheel with kerosene and wipe dry.
Will not start Starting motor does not operate	Discharged or damaged batteries Generator or alternator not operating properly Voltage or current regulator defective or out of adjustment Starting motor defective	Check batteries with hydrometer. Place weak batteries on charge, then check each cell under load. If cell voltage varies widely battery must be replaced as cell is shorted by sulphation or warped plates. Check brushes and connections to generator or alternator. Check alternator diodes. Replace defective units. Check adjustment of voltage and/or current regulators as instructed by the manufacturer. Replace defective regulator. Check starting motor. Replace if defective.
Will not start Distributor trouble	Dirt or water in distributor Burned rotor Burned points Defective condenser	Clean disributor cap and rotor. Check and replace rotor if necessary. If points are burned, replace points and condenser at the same time. Adjust points to proper gap.

TABLE 8
TROUBLESHOOTING - GASOLINE ENGINES

TROUBLE	PROBABLE CAUSE	REMEDY
Will not start Starter switch has no effect	Defective switch or solenoid Loose connections	Check switch, connections and solenoid. Replace if defective. Tighten connections.
Will not start Muffler plugged	Heavy carbon in muffler Baffle plates dislodged	Replace muffler.
Engine starts but misfires	Choke out	Push choke in,
	Carburetor needs adjustment	Adjust carburetor in accordance with manufacturer's instructions. Clean jets if necessary.
	Spark plugs with gaps too wide	Regap plugs with feeler gauge. Replace if necessary.
	Wrong type spark plug installed	Check plugs. Use only type specified by maunufacturer.
	Dirty spark plugs	Clean and regap or replace plugs.
	Dirty points	Clean and gap points. Replace points and condenser if necessary.
	Tappets out of adjustment	Adjust tappets for correct valve operation.
	Intake manifold loose	Remove manifold and check studs for damage. Replace.
	Valve stems worn	Replace valves. Normal on old engines.
Engine smooth at low speeds, rough and misfires at higher speeds.	High speed jet	Adjust high speed jet on carburetor for proper operation.
	Breaker points set too wide	Gap breaker points correctly.
	Spark plugs gapped too wide	Regap or replace plugs.
	Timing late	Recheck and adjust timing.
	Defective condenser	Replace condenser and points. Adjust properly.
	Cracked distributor	Replace broken unit.
Engine smooth at high speed but idles rough and misfires at low speed	Carburetor	Adjust idle jet on carburetor.
	Wrong octane rating of fuel	Use fuel of the proper grade.
	Fouled plugs	Caused by too rich mixture. Adjust idling mixture and clean, gap and replace plugs
	Low compression	Check for leaky valves and adjust or replace. Check engine gaskets for leaks. Replace gaskets. check ignition wiring. Replace if defective. Observe exhaust. Black smoke indicates too much oil in engine.

Basic Boat Maintenance - - J. Frank Brumbaugh

TABLE 8
TROUBLESHOOTING - GASOLINE ENGINES

TROUBLE	PROBABLE CAUSE	REMEDY
Engine overheats	Cooling water supply is inadequate	Check water pump. Replace if defective. Check water and wet exhaust lines for blockage or closed valves.
	Mixture too lean or rich	Adjust carburetor as specified by manufacturer. Heavy carbon inside engine must be removed.
	Retarded spark	Adjust distributor as specified by manufacturer.
	Muffler blocked	Replace muffler.
	Exhaust manifold water jacket leaks	Replace broken gasket. Pull up nuts on studs.
Engine backfires through carburetor	Needle valve	Adjust or replace carburetor needle valve.
	Dirt in jets	Clean jets. Check gasoline for sediment. Check air filter and clean or replace.
	Retarded spark	Adjust distributor as specified by manufacturer.
	Plug gaps wide	Regap and clean, or replace spark plugs.
	Blown cylinder gasket	Replace gasket. Use torque wrench to tighten nuts on head. Replace broken or damaged studs or nuts.
Engine backfires through exhaust	Exhaust valves	Check for bent stems, carbon in seat. Overhaul valves.
	Cylinders misfire	Remove and reinstall ignition harness so cylinders fire in the correct order.
Engine does not stop when ignition is turned off (dieseling)	Switch shorted	Replace switch.
	Plugs too hot	Use colder plugs
	Carbon on plugs or pistons	Check, clean and regap plugs. Pull head and scrape carbon from piston tops. Adjust carburetor for leaner mixture.

Basic Boat Maintenance - - J. Frank Brumbaugh

TABLE 8
TROUBLESHOOTING - GASOLINE ENGINES

TROUBLE	PROBABLE CAUSE	REMEDY
Engine seems to lack power	Poor compression	Check compression. Check valves, rings, gaskets, plugs. Check for carbon in cylinders. Replace defective parts. Engine may need overhaul.
	Mixture too lean	Adjust carburetor for richer mixture.
	Weak spark / Retarded spark	Check battery, distributor, coil and condenser. Charge battery if necessary. Replace condenser. Replace coil if necessary. Clean, adjust or replace distributor. Check all electrical wiring and replace if defective. Tighten electrical connections. Check timing and set if required.
	Valve timing	Check tappets for wear. Reset valves. Adjust locking nuts. Check valve clearance.
Engine lacks power / Water temperature increasing	Lack of cooling water	Check water pump and suction line. Clean water jacket out if necessary.
	Insufficient lubrication	Check crankcase level. Oil must be proper weight. Clear plugged oil lines. Replace dirty oil filters.
Shaft speed does not change when engine accelerates	Transmission	Overhaul transmission.
	Packing gland	Check that packing nut not set too tight. Check alignment.
	Propeller, strut	Check propeller strut for alignment and binding. Check that propeller is correct size and undamaged, not loose.
	Alignment	Check alignment of engine and shaft.
	Rudder	Check for bent or out-of-line rudder. Check rudder is not too close to propeller.
	Hull	Check bottom for excessive marine growth.
Engine starts / Oil pressure zero	Lack of oil	Fill crankcase. Check for broken oil line.
	Gauge or gauge line defective	Replace defective components.
	Defective pump	Check oil pump, lines, belts. Replace as required.
Engine operating / Oil pressure suddenly falls	Low oil supply / Broken or clogged oil lines	Fill crankcase. Replace or clear oil lines.
Engine operating / Oil pressure jumps, needle is erratic	Low oil supply / Pressure valve jammed	Fill crankcase. Check pressure valve.

Basic Boat Maintenance - - J. Frank Brumbaugh

TABLE 8
TROUBLESHOOTING - GASOLINE ENGINES

TROUBLE	PROBABLE CAUSE	REMEDY
Engine operating Low oil pressure	Oil too light Defective gauge or pressure valve Worn bearings	Drain crankcase and refill with proper weight oil. Replace defective gauge. Check pressure valve. Dismantle engine and check main bearings, and bearings on connecting rods.
Engine operating High oil pressure	Oil too heavy Lines clogged Defective gauge or pressure gauge	Drain crankcase and refill with proper weight oil. Clear clogged lines. Check or replace gauge and valve.

TABLE 9
TROUBLESHOOTING - DIESEL ENGINES

TROUBLE	PROBABLE CAUSE	REMEDY
Engine fails or is hard to start	Lack of juel Fuel valves closed Clogged fuel lines	Check fuel tank. Open valves. Clean clogged lines.
	Air entering fuel lines	Check fuel line connections and tighten. Replace broken gaskets. Bleed air from lines and close vents.
	Low compression	Check valves for seating and sticking, Replace leaky head gasket. Pull pistons and replace rings if necessary. Measure compression on each cylinder. Check those which register below the manufacturer's specifications.
	Blower on 2-cycle engine inoperative	Check for broken shaft, damaged driver parts. Replace.
	Low fuel pressure	Check that tanks contain proper weight fuel, not too thin. Clean filter. Check fuel pumps. Check fuel lines for breaks. Tighten fuel line connections.
	Starting battery weak	Check batteries. Recharge if required.
	Compressor not operating (on compressed air-starting engines)	Check air compressor, air lines, air tank.
Engine operates roughly and unevenly	Poor grade or wrong fuel type	Dump tanks and replace with proper fuel.
	Injector timing	Check and adjust timing in accordance with manufacturer's specifications.

Basic Boat Maintenance - - J. Frank Brumbaugh

TABLE 9
TROUBLESHOOTING - DIESEL ENGINES

TROUBLE	PROBABLE CAUSE	REMEDY
Engine does not seem to develop power	Spray nozzle	Inspect and clear clogged nozzles. This is most probable cause. Disconnect each injector in turn. Engine will lose power if diconnected injector is good but not if defective.
	Air entering fuel lines	Check and tighten fuel line connecitons. Replace defective gaskets on filters. Bleed air from lines and close vents.
	Injector tips	Check injectors for sticking valve plungers. Clean and reassemble.
	Injector pump valves	Check for sticking valves. Clean and replace.
	Worn rings, cylinders	Normal to much-used engines. Pull pistons. Replace rings. Rebore or insert new liners. Reassemble.
	Sticking valves	Caused by overheating. Clean. If distorted, regrind or replace.
	Exhaust pressure too high	Clean exhaust line. Replace muffler. Reduce flow of cooling water, if necessary.
	Fuel system	Check injectors, injector timing, fuel lines, air filter, fuel filter. Check for low compression. Follow manufacturer's recommendations.
Engine starts, then stops or stalls after a short time	Idle adjustment	Advance if Idle speed too low. Check governor.
	Water temperature too low.	Reduce supply of cooling water. Replace defective thermostat if used.
	Cylinders fail to fire properly	Check injectors, fuel pumps and lines.
	Fuel filters clogged	Clean fuel filters. If trouble recurs, fuel contains much dirt. Flush tanks and add fresh fuel.
Engine continues to run after stop control is tripped.	Control adjustment	Check and adjust stop control.
Engine operates Water temperature too high	Fresh water cooling system	Check and clear water lines. Replace water pumps. Replace thermostat. Clean heat exchanger.
Engine operates Oil temperature too high	Water cooling system	Check cooling system. Clean heat exchanger and oil coolers.
Engine knocks	Fuel metering Injectors	Check and adjust injectors and timing.

TABLE 9
TROUBLESHOOTING - DIESEL ENGINES

TROUBLE	PROBABLE CAUSE	REMEDY
Smoky exhaust is white	Cylinders misfiring	Check injectors, fuel pumps and lines.
Smoky exhaust is blue	Worn rings	Replace piston rings. May be necessary if engine is old to replace cylinder liner.
Smoky exhaust is brown or black	Injector timing Wrong fuel	Check that proper grade of fuel is used. Check and time injectors.

CHAPTER TEN
RODENTS AND INSECTS

Rodents -- mice and rats -- are rarely found on small boats unless they spend most of their time tied to a dock with no one aboard. While rodents are curious and may board an unused boat, this should be made as difficult as possible. There should be nothing aboard which would attract them. In the rare instances where a mouse or rat has taken up residence, the same remedies used ashore will be effective.

Rodents can jump sizable distances. They also can swim. When tied up and not in use your boat should be held away from the dock as far as possible with lines fore and aft leading to port and starboard. There should be no lines trailing into the water and the gangplank should be stowed away. Matches and foodstuffs on board should be enclosed in plastic containers not only to protect them from marauding rodents but to prevent food odors from attracting rodents. Mooring lines do provide a path for acrobatic rodents to board your boat, but this path will rarely be used unless rodents are attracted by food they can smell.

It is possible to rig rat shields on dock lines but this is not only difficult, it really looks laughable on anything smaller than a junior sized freighter. Such circular shields must be several feet in diameter to be effective. Fastened on half-inch dock lines they would not only appear incongruous but would probably cause damage to topsides at the usual small boat dock as they were moved about by the action of wind and waves. They would also create a stowage problem aboard most boats.

Boats which are visited daily or which are being lived on rarely will have a rodent problem. Noise and activity keep rodents at a distance, as will a pet cat kept aboard. Traps and poison bait are effective in ridding a boat of unwanted rodent stowaways, with the edge possibly going to poison. Rats, especially, are intelligent and trap-shy, although a well-baited and properly placed trap will generally catch mice with little difficulty.

Rodents tend to run along bulkheads, the edges of lockers, etc. They also will investigate anything which resembles a hole or tunnel. Set traps with the trigger end facing the bulkhead and almost touching it. Lean a board, cushion or other article against the bulkhead making a tent over the trap. Bacon is a much better bait than cheese, which is actually far less effective than folklore and legend would indicate. Tie the bacon to the bait pan with sewing thread, using several turns. This prevents the bait being stolen and almost forces a larcenous rodent to spring the trap while trying to remove the bait. Traps must be inspected daily, and reset or rebaited when necessary. Fresh bait should be used every day until all rodents have been trapped.

There are numerous poison baits available commercially. Not all are equally effective. One of the best is a dry product harmless to domestic animals. It looks much like rolled oat cereal. The active ingredient is a poison called *warfarin*, very effective against almost all rodents. (If you have a pet squirrel or rabbit aboard, don't use a poison bait of any kind. Squirrels and rabbits are rodents and will be killed should they ingest such poisons.) Warfarin is effective in very small amounts. Most rodent baits based on warfarin contain only about one percent of this poison. The poison is not detected by rodents and they will eat any such baits available. Water should be made available to them for drinking since the water speeds the action of the poison. Warfarin affects the circulatory system and effectively causes rodents to bleed to death internally. There is no blood externally to clean up afterwards. The bilges, lockers, compartments and all places in the boat where a rodent could hide should be inspected daily so dead bodies can be removed before they begin to decompose.

Insects are a much greater problem on small boats than are rodents. Here, again, prevention is much easier than the cure. Basically there are only four varieties of insect which are apt to cause problems: ants, cockroaches, flies, and mosquitoes.

Ants can come aboard a boat tied up to a pier. They can also be brought aboard in stores, particularly packaged and fresh foods. Foods properly stored in closed, airtight containers will be protected from insects and will not attract them. Crumbs and spills will attract them and thus should be cleaned up. A spotless, odor-free galley will seldom be visited by ants. Any of the commercially available ant poisons will be effective. So will spray insecticides, but these must not be a type containing a solvent which will soften the plastics used in fiberglass boat construction. Before using insecticide sprays -- or any aerosol product -- on a fiberglass boat, check with the boat manufacturer to ascertain which products will be safe to use.

Cockroaches and their oversized tropical cousins (they are euphemistically called "palmetto bugs" in the south) are nearly impossible to keep off a boat. They come aboard on dock lines, board over your gangplank, hide among stores brought aboard, and the larger varieties, up to several inches long, have well developed wings and are strong fliers. They are also expert swimmers. When they decide to board your boat, they will arrive. It is best to expect them and to be ready for them.

Keep the inside of the boat as dry as possible, especially in the galley and head, since roaches like dampness. Spray likely hiding places once each week with an effective roach killer such as *Raid, Black Flag* or similar insecticides, even if you never see a roach. (For every roach you see there are ten others waiting in the wings.) Be sure the insecticide will not stain or damage the areas sprayed.

One of the simplest and least expensive means of preventing a roach infestation of your boat, and which will kill any roaches now aboard, is to sprinkle *Boric Acid* powder, obtainable at any drug store, along the base of bulkheads, inside lockers and bins, behind and under drawers, etc. Make sure it is powder, not boric acid crystals. Roaches do not recognize boric acid powder as a poison. As they walk through it, some powder clings to their legs and abdomen. As they groom themselves they ingest some of the powder, which soon kills them. Being cannibalistic, live roaches will eat their dead comrades and soon will join them in death.

Very little powder is needed if sprinkled along those places roaches tend to walk and hide. Should it become damp -- you will smell a "clean" odor -- merely clean the old powder up and sprinkle fresh powder in place.

Boric acid powder will last for months or years and keep on killing any roaches which may come aboard, as long as it remains dry so it can coat the legs and abdomens of roaches walking through it. Two weeks after first distributing boric acid powder, and often much sooner, there will be no live roaches aboard your boat.

There are several roach poisons available which will keep the roach population under control. *Lucky Mac* is one of the most effective when used according to directions on the package, and there are others which come in pill form which also work well. Roach poisons should be set out and used in conjunction with the spraying of insecticide since they are mutually advantageous in roach control.

A particularly bad infestation of roaches can only be brought under control by fumigation. This is best done by a professional exterminator who will guarantee his work, such as *Orkin, Terminex* and others. There are, however, fumigants commercially available which you can safely use provided the directions are followed exactly. These come in pressurized, aerosol cans with valves designed so once activated to release the contents they cannot be turned off.

To fumigate your boat properly with an aerosol fumigant, the entire below decks area must be closed and made as airtight as possible, and all enclosed areas opened so the poison gas can penetrate. Open all locker and compartment doors and lids. Prop berth mattresses and cushions up against bulkheads or sides. Open all drawers part way or remove them entirely. Lift removable floor boards., Open the hatch between the cabin and engine compartment. Close all ports, windows and the forward hatch. Stuff rags into all ventilators and blower air lines. Stuff rags or paper into all non-closable Dorade hatch covers. Spread several layers of newspapers on the cabin sole and set the can of fumigant in the center of the papers.

Read -- and understand -- the directions printed on the can of fumigant. When all is ready and the below decks area as completely airtight as possible with only the main hatch left open, activate the valve on the can. The gas will form a visible spray extending vertically.

Do not let this spray, which may extend upwards two or three feet, hit you in the face. When the spray starts, immediately get back on deck and close the main hatch as tightly as possible. Leave the boat for several hours if you can; otherwise stay on the windward side so you will not be exposed to fumigant gas which may leak out from below.

    After several hours, at least as long as suggested by the directions on the can of fumigant, open all hatches and remove plugs from ventilators. Powered ventilators may be operated. Do not go below to open windows and ports since there will still be fumigant gas present for an hour or more after ventilation has begun. Allow sufficient time for all gas to dissipate before spending much time below. After an hour or two it will be safe to go below to quickly open windows and ports, returning topsides as soon as possible. You should, if possible, allow the ventilation system several hours or even overnight to clear out the gas before considering the cabin completely safe for normal occupancy.

    If the boat was badly infested with roaches prior to being fumigated, you will find their bodies lying all over everything. Sweep them up with broom and dust pan and dump them over the side. Pay attention to the inside of drawers, lockers and compartments, the bilges, underneath bottom drawers, and in all the various nooks and crannies, and remove the dead bodies. Since fumigation may not kill all unhatched eggs it should be repeated in seven to ten days. Fumigant spray is available in cans selling for approximately $5.00, and two to four cans is usually sufficient for the average pleasure boat.

    Flies and mosquitoes which manage to get aboard are best controlled by insecticide strips such as the *Shell No-Pest Strip,* and other similar solid insecticides. These strips of plastic are impregnated with a very effective insecticide which is released gradually over a 90-day period, after which the strips should be discarded and new ones installed. Each strip protects a volume of approximately 1000 cubic feet, or about as much space as is below decks in the average 28-foot sail boat or interior space in a 24-foot power cruiser. Other types of aerosol spray insecticides can be used, of course, if they do not stain the interior of the boat. However, they are not long-lasting and their odor is sometimes objectionable. The insecticide strips produce no discernible odor when used according to directions, though a mild odor can be detected if the strip itself is sniffed. The strips are claimed to be harmless to human beings and pets, while most spray insecticides carry warnings on the label not to inhale the spray.

Everything possible should be done to prevent insects from coming aboard. Even though it may be impossible to be 100 percent effective you can easily keep invasions to manageable proportions. All ports and windows which open must be screened. Either bronze wire screening or fiberglass mesh is suitable and long-lasting. Ventilator openings must be screened. Holes, slots and cutouts which ventilate lockers and other enclosed spaces must be screened. All drains which pass through the hull above the waterline should either be fitted with rubber or leather flaps to keep them closed when not in use, or plugs fitted so they may be installed in their inboard ends. Drains which are fitted with pumps or water traps need no other protection against insects.

The forehatch and main companionway hatch openings must be protected by screening when they are opened in areas where flying insects abound. The simplest way of doing an effective job of screening these openings is by making fitted screens of mosquito netting or fiberglass screen edged with *Velcro* strips. Matching *Velcro* strips should be permanently fixed all around the edges of the openings with adhesive or double-sided tape. *Velcro* strips are sold in pairs, one portion consisting of a multitude of tiny plastic hooks and the other of small plastic loops. When pressed together, the hooks mesh with the loops and remain in place until pulled apart. Usually the strip of loops is permanently attached around the opening and the hooked strip sewn to the edges of the screening material. Such screens are simple to make and use, and are easy to stow when not needed.

Flies and mosquitoes, except for the few which may already be aboard, are rarely encountered far from land. If you anchor some distance offshore, or in an area where there is an onshore wind, they will seldom be noticed. It is only when docked or when anchored close to shore that flies and mosquitoes may seek you out.

Most ants and roaches can be prevented from coming aboard with stores if care is taken. Unpack all stores, groceries, etc. on the dock or in the dinghy. Inspect them for insects before placing them aboard your boat. Shake out all bags before taking them aboard. Cardboard boxes should never be brought on board your boat since their bottom flaps may, and very often do, harbor insects or their eggs. Since roaches are the most important insect to be kept off your boat, kill every one you see. Step on them or otherwise make sure they are dead. It is of no use to flip them into the water. Roaches are excellent swimmers and will quite happily swim to your boat and clamber aboard. It is next to impossible to drown them. Remember, ashore they thrive in sink and bathtub drains and the water does not appear to faze them. So kill them if you want to keep them off your boat.

Moths can be a problem if you have woolen clothing or blankets aboard. There are numerous synthetic fiber materials which are entirely mothproof and which are excellent substitutes for wool, even in extremely cold weather. *Orlon* is ideal for blankets and sweaters, and even for coats. *Nylon* is often used for windbreakers and jackets. Synthetic blends are ideal for clothing. Cotton which is used mainly in sheets, cases and towels, is not attractive to moths.

Woolen materials can be mothproofed by commercial dry cleaning establishments each time they are cleaned. This should be done if you feel woolens are desirable to have aboard. There are also numerous moth repellents available, such as the familiar -- and odorous -- moth balls and naphthalene flakes. They work well but their odor is distasteful in the small enclosure of a boat's cabin and will not be appreciated by anyone who becomes seasick.

A better solution is to line the interior of the woolen locker with cedar. Thin, aromatic cedar boards with tongue-and-groove edges and ends are available from many lumber yards and some large department stores. These are easy to install and can be glued in place or nailed, using thin wire brads. Do not attempt to nail anything to fiberglass, however. Cedar linings must never be painted, varnished or waxed. They must be left natural so the oils in the wood can vaporize and repel moths. They may be washed when dirty, using a mild detergent and fresh water, though this should rarely if ever be necessary if woolens are kept reasonably clean.

APPENDIX ONE
LIST OF ILLUSTRATIONS

Figure 1 Battery Log

Figure 2 Engine Hours Log

Figure 3 Locking Stitch

Figure 4 Running Stitch

Figure 5 Round Stitch

Figure 6 Herringbone Stitch

Figure 7 Repairing a Ripped Sail

Figure 8 Sewn Grommet

Figure 9 Wire Cable Splice, Simplified

Figure 10 Ratlines

Figure 11 Bosun's Chair Hoisting Tackle

Figure 12 Bosun's Chair Construction

Figure 13 Hydrometer

Figure 14 Edge Padding With Rope

Figure 15 Ventilators

Figure 16 Patching Holes in Fiberglass Hulls

APPENDIX TWO
LIST OF TABLES

Table 1 Daily Preventive Maintenance

Table 2 Weekly Preventive Maintenance

Table 3 Monthly Preventive Maintenance

Table 4. Annual or Start of Cruise Preventive Maintenance

Table 5 Wire Sizes for DC Circuits

Table 6 Wire Sizes for AC circuits

Table 7 Storage Life of Commonly Used Foods

Table 8 Troubleshooting Gasoline Engines

Table 9 Troubleshooting Diesel Engines

Basic Boat Maintenance - - *J. Frank Brumbaugh*

APPENDIX THREE
TOOLS & SUPPLIES

This list has been compiled through the joint effort of our staff and many contributing writers.

As you delve deeper into boating, you will always find a need for one more tool, or a few more supplies. It is truly a case of "Too much is never enough and enough is always too much." With this in mind it is best to adapt the following to your boat's needs and storage capacity.

The boat tools should not be shared with the car or the home. Purchase a good quality plastic tool box larger than the current need. Remove the handle which will certainly come off when you are transferring the box to the boat or the dock. A second box for less used tools is also a good idea.

* Tools for a small cruising sailboat without electrical or plumbing systems.

** Tools to add to the list for a mid-sized cruiser with electrical, plumbing, electronics and an inboard engine.

*** Tools for the long-term cruiser or liveaboard sailor intending to make most of the repairs to most of the systems.

The balance of the list will be needed at your land base for extensive repairs, renovations, upgrades and restoration projects.

HAND TOOLS

Good brands will carry a life time warranty.
* # 1, #2, #3 Phillips screwdrivers.
* Thin blade 3/16", medium blade 1/4", heavy blade 3/8" straight screwdrivers.

All the above should also be purchased in the stubby length.
** Jewelers set of screwdrivers.
** Various square drivers if you have this type of fastener on your boat. You will have to know the sizes you will need.
* Linesman pliers.
** Dikes/side cutters.
** Wire strippers. Buy the type with the stripper portion before the hinge.
** Terminal crimps.
** Digital multi-meter.
* Long-nose pliers.
** Needle-nose pliers.
* Vise Grips
* Small slip joint pliers (opens to 2").
*** Straight blade sheet metal cutters.
** Caulk gun.
*** Lufkin folding rule with brass slide extension.
** Large and small metal files.
* Set of allen wrenches 1/16" to 7/16" minimum.
*** China bristles paint brushes with an angle cut, in sizes 1", 1-1/2", 2", 2-1/2".
** School pencils.
** Pencil sharpener.
** Thin blade awl.
* 8" & 12" adjustable wrench.
** 12" Lenox hacksaw with 18, 24, & 32 teeth per inch

blades.
** Estwing leather handle straight claw hammer.
*** A #2, & #3 nail set.
** Combination wrench set.
** 1/4" drive socket set.
* 3/8" drive socket set.
** Ignition wrench set.
The term "set" is used because most of these tools are sold in sets. You can purchase them individually but you will spend more than buying a set.
** 24" to 36" adjustable wrench. The size will depend on the prop nut size of your boat.
** Battery carrying strap.
** Feeler gauges (blade type).
** Cordless drill with two batteries, charger, cobalt drill bits ranging from 1/32" to 3/8" and screwdriver bits with a good holder. These should be the same size as your hand screwdrivers.
** Large slip joint pliers (opens to 4").
*** 2# Ballpeen hammer.
Caulking iron.
*** Rubber mallet.
*** Small & large Wonder bars.
*** Diston small dovetail saw.
*** Diston coping saw.
*** Diston 13 point hand saw.
*** Stanley 25' tape measure.
*** Stanley combination square.
*** Stanley #40 wood chisels 1/2", 3/4", 1".
*** Block plane.
*** Half round wood file/rasp.
*** Heavy blade awl.
*** Larger size drill bits 7/16" to 1" forsener bits are the best for large wood bits. Metal bits should be cobalt.
*** Brad point bits 1/16" to 3/8".

Plug cutters 3/8" to 3/4"
*** Hole saw set.
*** Metal chisel and drift set.
** Right angle-straight and Phillips screwdrivers.
** Fish tape.
** Heavy gauge terminal crimp tool.
** Line wrench set.
** 1/2" drive socket set.
** Deep well socket set for all the different size drives you now own. Some of these may have been included when you purchased the sets.
*** 1/2" Breaker bar.
*** 1/2" Click stop torque wrench.
** 1/2" drive large sockets for all the bolts/nuts which are larger than the sets contain.
** Wrenches for the same bolts/nuts.

POWER TOOLS

Purchase brand name, heavy duty, commercial grade tools with a high ampere draw. These are the only tools that will last.
3/8" & 1/2" power drills.
Circular saw with good carbide tooth blades.
*** Random orbiting sander with 5" & 6" pads. Buy your 3M gold sanding disk in the 6" size and cut them down when you need the 5" size. Buy rolls of these grits. 60, 80, 100, 120, 150, 180.
Power miter box with an 80 tooth carbide blade.
3" x 24" or 4" x 24" belt sander. Buy at least three belts of each of these grits. 36, 80, 100, 120.
*** Soldering gun with electrical solder and flux.
Heat gun.
*** Random orbit buffer if you own a fiberglass boat.
Scrolling jigsaw with various wood and metal blades.

Router with various bits purchased as the jobs warrant. Always use roller bearing bits where applicable.
*** Sawz-all with various size and types of blades for wood/metal.
Biscuit jointer with at least two hundred of the two larger size biscuits.
*** 25', 50', & 75' #12 wire extension cords.
Table or radial arm saw. The radial arm saw can be set up with a multitude of attachments to handle many different functions other than cross cutting and ripping.

SUPPLIES

All Stainless Steel Fasteners

** At least 50 each of these Phillips head screws.
#4 x 1/2", 3/4", 1" Flat and oval head.
#6 x 1/2", 3/4", 1", 1-1/4", 1-1/2", 1-3/4", 2" Flat and oval head.
#8, #10, #12 Same as #6 plus 2-1/2", 3" Flat and oval head.
** Finish washers for each of the above size screw numbers.
#6, #8, #10, 1/2", 3/4", 1", 1-1/2" Pan head.
** At least 10 each of these fasteners.
1/4" x 20 x 2", 3", 4" Flat and stove head bolts with 2 washers and 1 nut each.
5/16" & 3/8" x 1", 1-1/2", 2", 2-1/2", 3" machine bolts with 2 washers and 1 nut each.
** Cap nuts for each of the above sizes.
*** 1/4" x 2", 3", 4", 5" lag bolts with washers.
** Large fender washers for each of the above sizes.
*** 2 pieces of solid rod 3' long in 1/4", 3/8", 1/2".

*** 2 pieces of threaded rod 3' long with 6 nuts and washers per piece in 1/4", 3/8", 1/2".
* Various size cotter pins to replace ones which will need to be removed. Check the sizes you need before ordering or purchase a cotter pin kit with various sizes included.
18 gauge brass or stainless steel brads in 1/2", 3/4", 1"

ELECTRICAL

** Butt terminals, male and female quick disconnect terminals. Order at least 50 each for wire gauges, 22-18, 16-14, 12-10, 8.
** Spade connectors, stud connectors. Order at least 50 each for the same gauge of wire above to fit around stud sizes 4-6, 8-10, 1/4", 5/16", 3/8".
*** 10 terminals for each size battery cable in use on your boat.
** 6 battery clamps (lugs, the kind used on your car) with stud. Do not connect the battery wires directly to the clamp; use the stud and terminals.
** 200 each of 6" & 11" medium duty wire ties.
*** 100 each of 3/4" and 1-1/2" cable clamps.
*** 1 each 4, 6, 8, 10 position terminal blocks. 6 each 20 amp in-line fuse holders with 5 each of, 5 amp, 10 amp, 15 amp, & 20 amp fuses.
*** 100 ft each of wire gauges 18, 16, 14, 12, 10, 8. Tinned marine primary wire.
*** 25 ft each of wire gauges 6 & 4.
*** 10 butt connectors for 6 & 4 wire.
*** 10 ft of battery cable for each size you have in use on board.
*** 2 ft each of heat shrink tubing 3/16", 1/4", 3/8", 1/2," 3/4".

MISC. ELECTRICAL SUPPLIES

** Liquid electrical tape.
** Vinyl electrical tape.
** Nylon string to use as a wire fishing device.
** 1 Pair of battery jumper cables. They must be long enough to reach between the banks of batteries you may need to jump. If you can not find them this long, make up your own with heavy ends and # 2 battery cable.
** Jumper wires for testing. These can be made with 4 alligator clips and 12 gauge wire.
** 1 breaker or fuse holder for each different size and type you on have board.
** 1 fuse for each specialty fuse on board.
** 1 switch for each type on board.
** 2 extra bulbs for each type on board.
** 1 lamp socket for each type on board.
*** 1 of each shore line end or an extra 50' shore line set.
** 1 connector for each type of electronic instrument connector on board.

SEALANTS, PAINT, AND REPAIR PRODUCTS

** 1 tube each of Teak Deck Systems, 3M 5200 in white, GE silicone in white & clear, Star Bright polysulfide underwater sealant, Sea Repair.
** 1 small kit each of Epoxy, Marine Tex, Boat Yard fiberglass with 6 oz. cloth and matching gel coat colors.
*** 1 qt each of varnish, top sides paint for each color on board, stain, paint thinner, acetone, lacquer thinner, Penatrol, boiled linseed oil.

*** Coffee cans.
*** Plastic pots in 1 qt size.
*** Disposable brushes in 1/2", 1", 1-1/2", 2", 2-1/2".

PLUMBING PARTS

* The best method of determining your needs for plumbing will be to go through your supply and waste systems measuring each hose, clamp, tubing and fitting type and size. With this list in hand purchase at least two of each type of fitting, 10 of each size clamp, hose to replace the longest length of each size or fittings and hose to patch in the very long lengths. As with your shore power line, carry an extra water supply hose of no less than 50'. Also purchase water hose repair ends.

** This may not be considered plumbing by some, but it carries water, therefore it is included in this section. Your engines have many small sizes and lengths of hoses. As with the plumbing hoses, buy enough to replace the longest length of each size with the proper size clamps. These should be the heavy wall hose with wire reinforcement.

** If you have large exhaust lines you do not need to carry a full length. Do carry a large coffee can with 4 hose clamps which are a larger size than the exhaust hose. You must carry at least one spare impeller or a rebuilding kit with the impeller included for every pump on board. THIS IS A MUST!

MISC. SUPPLIES

* Shock cords and ends.
* Buckets.
* Sponges.
* Chamois.

Basic Boat Maintenance - - J. Frank Brumbaugh

- ** Toilet brush.
- ** Scrub brush.
- ** Deck brush with handle.
- *** Roller handle, pan and pads.
- ** Bronze wool.
- ** Bronze scrub brush.
- ** Detergents.
- ** Cleaning products.
- ** Polishes.
- ** Compounds.
- ** Water resistant/proof glue.
- *** Extension cord ends.
- ** Patching material for every inflatable on board.
- ** Repair parts for engine(s).
- *** Antifreeze.
- ** Oils.
- ** Grease gun with grease.
- ** Transmission fluid.
- * 5 gals of extra fuel.
- * Duct tape.
- * Riggers tape.
- *** Masking tape.
- *** Sheet sand paper in grits 50, 80, 100, 120, 150, 180, 220. At least 5 sheets of each grit.
- * At least two complete sets of dock lines and anchor rodes.
- * One 3/4" line (regardless of boat size to 45') three times the length of the boat. (Tow line)

APPENDIX FOUR
GLOSSARY

This glossary has been compiled through a joint effort of the staff of Bristol Fashion Publications and many authors. It is not intended to cover the many thousands of words and terms in the language exclusive to boating. The longer you are around boats and boaters, the more of this language you will learn.

A

Accumulator tank - A tank used to add air pressure to the freshwater system thus reducing water pump run time.
Aft - Near the stern.
Amidships - Midway between the bow and the stern.
Antifouling - Bottom paint used to prevent growth on the boat bottom.
Athwartships - Any line running at a right angle to the fore/aft centerline.

B

Backer plate- Metal plate used to increase the strength of a through bolt application, such as with the installation of a cleat.
Ballast - Weight added to improve a boat's sea handling abilities of the boat or to counterbalance an unevenly loaded boat.

Beam - The widest point of the boat.

Bilge - The lowest point inside a boat.

Bilge pump - Underwater water pump used to remove water from the bilge.

Binnacle - A box or stand used to hold the compass.

Bolt - Any fastener with any head style and machine thread shank.

Boot stripe - Contrasting trim paint of a contrasting color located just above the bottom paint on the hull sides.

Breaker - Replaces a fuse to interrupt power on an electrical circuit when that circuit becomes overloaded or shorted.

Bridge - The steering station of a boat.

Brightwork - Polished metal or varnished wood aboard a boat.

Bristol Fashion - The highest standard of condition any vessel can obtain and the highest state of crew seamanship. The publishing company that brought you this book.

Bulkhead - A wall running across (athwartships) the boat.

Butt connectors - A type of crimp connector used to join two wires end to end in a continuing run of the wire.

C

Canvas - A general term used to describe cloth used for boat coverings. A type of cloth material.

Carlin - A structural beam joining the inboard ends of deck beams that are cut short around a mast or hatch.

Cavitation - Reduced propeller efficiency due to vapor pockets in areas of low pressure on the blades. Turbulence caused by prop rotation that reduces the efficiency of the prop.

Centerboard - A hinged board or plate at the bottom of a sailboat of shallow draft. It reduces leeway under sail.

Chafing gear - Any material used to prevent the abrasion of another material.

Chain - Equally sized inter-looping oblong rings commonly used for anchor rode.

Chain locker - A forward area of the vessel used for chain storage.

Chine - The intersection of the hull side with the hull bottom, usually in a moderate-speed to fast hull. Sailboats and displacement-speed powerboats usually have a round bilge and do not have a chine. Also, the turn of the hull below the waterline on each side of the boat. A sailboat hull, displacement hull and semi-displacement hull have a round chine. Planing hulls all have a hard (sharp corner) chine.

Chock - A metal fitting used in mooring or rigging to control the turn of the lines.

Cleat - A device used to secure a line aboard a vessel or on a dock.

Clevis - A Y-shaped piece of sailboat hardware about two to four inches long that connects a wire rope rigging terminal to one end of a turnbuckle.

Coaming - A barrier around the cockpit of a vessel to prevent water from washing into the cockpit.

Cockpit - Usually refers to the steering area of a sailboat or the fishing area of a sport-fishing boat. The sole of this area is always lower than the deck.

Companionway - An entrance into a boat or a stairway from one level of a boat's interior to another.

Cribbing - Large blocks of wood used to support the boat's hull during it's time on land.

Cutlass Bearing® - A rubber tube that is sized to a

propeller shaft and fits inside the propeller shaft strut.

D

Davit - Generally used to describe a lifting device for a dinghy.
Delaminate - A term used to describe two or more layers of any adhered material that have separated from each other because of moisture or air pockets in the laminate.
Device - A term used in conjunction with electrical systems. Generally used to describe lights, switches receptacles, etc.
Dinghy - Small boat used as a tender to the mother ship.
Displacement - The amount of water, in weight, displaced by the boat when floating.
Displacement Hull - A hull that has a wave crest at bow and stern and settles in the wave trough in the middle. A boat supported by its own ability to float while underway.
Dock - Any land based structure used for mooring a boat.
Draft - The distance from the waterline to the keel bottom. The amount of space (water) a boat needs between its waterline and the bottom of the body of water. When a boat's draft is greater than the water depth, you are aground.
Dry rot - This is not a true term as the decay of wood actually occurs in moist conditions.

F

Fairing - The process of smoothing a portion of the boat so it will present a very even and smooth surface after the finish is applied.

Fairing compound - The material used to achieve the fairing process.

Fairlead - A portion of rigging used to turn a line, cable or chain to increase the radius of the turn and thereby reduce friction.

Fall - The portion of a block and tackle system that moves up or down.

Fastening - Generally used to describe a means by which the planking is attached to the boat structure. Also used to describe screws, rivets, bolts, nails etc. (fastener)

Fiberglass - Clothlike material made from glass fibers and used with resin and hardener to increase the resin strength.

Filter - Any device used to filter impurities from any liquid or air.

Fin keel - A keel design that often resembles an up-side-down "T" when viewed from fore or aft.

Flame arrestor - A safety device placed on top of a gasoline carburetor to stop the flame flash of a backfiring engine.

Flat head - A screw head style that can be made flush with or recessed into the wood surface.

Float switch - An electrical switch commonly used to automatically control the on-off of a bilge pump. When this device is used, the pump is considered to be an automatic bilge pump.

Flying bridge - A steering station high above the deck level of the boat.

Fore - The front of a boat.

Fore-and-aft - A line running parallel to the keel. The keel runs fore-and-aft.

Forecastle - The area below decks in the forwardmost section. (pronunciation is often fo'c's'le)

Foredeck - The front deck.

Forward - Any position in front of amidships.

Freeboard - The distance on the hull from the waterline to the deck level.

Full keel - A keel design with heavy lead ballast and deep draft. This keel runs from the bow, to the stern at the rudder.

G

Galley - Kitchen.

Gelcoat - A hard, shiny coat over a fiberglass laminate that keeps water from the structural laminate.

Gimbals - A method of supporting anything that must remain level regardless of the boat's attitude.

Grommet - A ring pressed into a piece of cloth through which a line can be run.

Gross tonnage - The total interior space of a boat.

Ground tackle - Refers to the anchor, chain, line and connections as one unit.

H

Hanging locker - A closet with a rod for hanging clothes.

Hatch - An opening with a lid that open in an upward direction.

Hauling - Removing the boat from the water. The act of pulling on a line or rode is also called hauling.

Hawsehole - A hull opening for mooring lines or anchor rodes.

Hawsepipes - A pipe through the hull, for mooring or anchor rodes.

Head - Toilet. Also refers to the entire area of the bathroom.

Helm - The steering station and steering gear.

Holding tank - Used to hold waste for disposal ashore.

Hose - Any flexible tube capable of carrying a liquid.

Hull - The structure of a vessel not including any component other than the shell.

Hull lines - The drawing of the hull shape in plan, profile and sections (body plan).

I

Inboard - Positioned toward the center of the boat. An engine mounted inside the boat.

K

Keel - A downward protrusion running fore and aft on the center line of any boat's bottom. It is the main structural member.

King plank - The plank on the center line of a wooden laid deck.

Knees - A structural member reinforcing and connecting two other structural members. Also, two or more vertical beams at the bow of a tugboat used to push barges.

L

Launch - To put a boat into the water.

Lazarette - A storage compartment in the stern of a boat.

Lead - The material used for ballast.

Limber holes - Holes in the bilge timbers to allow water to run to the lowest part of the bilge, where it can be pumped out.

LOA - Length Over All. The over all length of a boat.

Locker - A storage area.

Log - A tube or cylinder through which a shaft or rudder stock runs from the inside to the outside. The log will have a packing gland (stuffing box) on the inside of the boat. Speed log is used to measure distance traveled. A book used to a keep record of the events on board a boat.

LWL - Length on the Waterline. The length of a boat at the water line.

M

Manifold - A group of valves connected by piping to tanks to allow filling and removal from one or more tanks.

Marine gear - Boat's transmission.

Mast - An upward pointing timber used as the sail's main support. Also used on power and sailboats to mount flags, antennas and lights.

Mile - A statute mile (land mile) is 5280 feet. A nautical mile (water mile) or knot is 6080.2 feet.

Mizzen mast - The aftermost mast on a sailboat.

N

Nautical mile - A distance of 6080.2 feet

Navigation lights - Lights required to be in operation while underway at night. The lighting pattern varies with the type, size and use of the vessel.

Nut - A threaded six-sided device used in conjunction with a bolt.

Nylon - A material used for lines when some give is desirable. Hard nylon is used for plumbing and rigging fittings.

O

Oval head - A screw head used when the head can only be partially recessed. The raised (oval) portion of the head will remain above the surface.

Overhangs - The length from the bow or stern ending of the waterline to the forward or aft end of the hull.

P

Painter - A line used to tow or secure a small boat or dinghy.

Pan head - A screw head with a flat surface, used when the head will remain completely above the surface.

Panel - A term used to describe the main electrical distribution point, usually containing the breakers or fuses.

Pier - Same general use as a dock.

Pile - A concrete or wooden post driven or otherwise embedded into the water's bottom.

Piling - A multiple structure of piles.

Pipe - A rigid, thick-walled tube.

Planing hull - A hull design, which under sufficient speed, will rise above it's dead-in-the-water position and seem to ride on the water.

Planking - The covering members of a wooden structure.

Plug - A type of pipe, tubing or hose fitting. Describes any device used to stop water from entering the boat through the hull. A cylindrical piece of wood placed in a screw hole to hide the head of the screw.

Port - A land area for landing a boat. The left side when facing forward.

Propeller (Prop, Wheel, Screw) - Located at the end of the shaft. The prop must have at least two blades and propels the vessel through the water with a screwing motion.

R

Radar - A electronic instrument which can be used to "see" objects as blips on a display screen.

Rail - A non-structural safety member on deck used as a banister to help prevent falling overboard.

Reduction gear - The gear inside the transmission housing that reduces the engine rpm to a propeller shaft Rpm that is optimum for that hull and engine.

Ribs - Another term for frames. The planking is fastened to these structural members.

Rigging - Generally refers to any item placed on the boat after the delivery of the vessel from the manufacturer. Also refers to all the wire rope, line, blocks, falls and other hardware needed for sail control.

Ring terminals - A crimp connector with a ring that can have a screw placed inside the ring for a secure connection.

Rode - Anchor line or chain.

Rope - A term that refers to cordage and this term is only used only on land. When any piece of cordage is on board a boat, it is referred to as line or one of it's more designating descriptions.

Round head - A screw or bolt head with a round surface that remains completely above the material being fastened.

Rudder - Located directly behind the prop and used to control the steering.

Rudder stock - Also known as rudder post. A piece of round, solid metal attached to the rudder at one end and the steering quadrant at the other.

S

Samson post - A large piece of material extending from the keel upward through the deck and used to secure lines for mooring or anchoring.

Screw - A threaded fastener. A term for propeller.

Screw thread - A loosely spaced, coarse thread used for wood and sheet metal screws.

Sea cock - A valve used to control the flow of water from the sea to the device it is supplying.

Shackle - A metal link with a pin to close the opening. Commonly used to secure the anchor to the rode.

Shaft - A solid metal cylinder that runs from the marine gear to the prop. The prop is mounted on the end of the shaft.

Shear pin - A small metal pin that inserted through the shaft and propeller on small boats. If the prop hits a hard object, the pin will "shear" without causing severe damage to the shaft.

Sheaves - The rolling wheel in a pulley.

Sheet metal screw - Any fastener that has a fully threaded shank of wood screw threads.

Ship - Any seagoing vessel. To ship an item on a boat means to bring it aboard.

Shock cord - An elastic line used to dampen the shock stress of a load.

Slip - A docking space for a boat. A berth.

Sole - The cabin and cockpit floor.

Spade rudder - A rudder that is not supported at its bottom.

Stability - The ability of a hull to return to level trim after being heeled by the forces of wind or water.

Stanchion - A metal post that holds the lifelines or railing along the deck's edge.

Starboard - The right side when facing forward.

Statute mile - A land mile. 5280 feet.

Stem - The forwardmost structural member of the hull.

Step - The base of the mast where the mast is let into the keel or mounted on the keel in a plate assembly.

Stern - The back .

Strut - A metal supporting device for the shaft.

Stuffing box - The interior end of the log where packing is inserted to prevent water intrusion from the shaft or rudder stock.

Surveyor - A person who inspects the boat for integrity and safety.

Switch - Any device, except breakers, that interrupts the flow of electrical current to a device.

T

Tachometer - A instrument used to count the revolutions of anything turning, usually the engine, marine gear or shaft.

Tack rag - A rag with a sticky surface used to remove dust before applying a finish to any surface.

Tank - Any large container that holds a liquid.

Tapered plug - A wooden dowel tapered to a blunt point and is inserted into a seacock or hole in the hull in an emergency.

Tender - A small boat (dinghy) used to travel between shore and the mother ship. A boat with limited stability is said to be tender.

Terminal lugs - Car-style, battery cable ends.

Through hull (Thru hull) - Any fitting between the sea and the boat that goes "through" the hull material.

Tinned wire - Stranded copper wire with a tin additive to prevent corrosion.

Topsides - Refers to being on deck. The part above the waterline.

Torque (or Torsion) - The rotating force on a shaft. (lb-in)

Transmission - Refers to a marine or reduction gear.

Transom - The flat part of the stern.

Trim - The attitude with which the vessel floats or moves through the water.

Trip line - A small line made fast to the anchor crown.

When weighing anchor this line is pulled to back the anchor out and thus release the anchor's hold in the bottom.

Tubing - A thin-walled metal or plastic cylinder, similar to pipe but having thinner walls.

Turn of the bilge - A term used to refer to the corner of the hull where the vertical hull sides meet the horizontal hull bottom.

Turnbuckles - In England, they are called bottle screws. They secure the wire rope rigging to the hull and are used to adjust the tension in the wire rope.

V

Valves - Any device that controls the flow of a liquid.

Vessel - A boat or ship.

VHF radio - The electronic radio used for short-range (10 to 20 mile maximum) communications between shore and vessels and between vessels.

W

Wake - The movement of water as a result of a vessel's movement through the water.

Washer - A flat, round piece of metal with a hole in the center. A washer is used to increase the holding power of a bolt and nut by distributing the stress over a larger area.

Waste pump - Any device used to pump waste.

Waterline - The line created at the intersection of the vessel's hull and the water's surface. A horizontal plane through a hull that defines the shape on the hull lines. The actual waterline or just waterline, is the height at that the boat floats. If weight is added to the boat, it floats at a deeper waterline.

Water pump - Any device used to pump water.

Wheel - Another term for prop or the steering wheel.

Whipping - Any method used, except a knot, to prevent a line end from unraveling.

Winch - A device used to pull in or let out line or rode. It is used to decrease the physical exertion needed to do the same task by hand.

Windlass - A type of winch used strictly with anchor rode.

Woodscrew - A fastener with only two-thirds of the shank threaded with a screw thread.

Y

Yacht - A term used to describe a pleasure boat, generally over twenty-five feet. Usually used to impress someone.

Yard - A place where boats are stored and repaired.

Z

Zebra mussel - A small, freshwater mussel that will clog anything in a short period of time.

Books Published by Bristol Fashion Publications

www.wescottcovepublishing.com

Boat Repair Made Easy — Haul Out
Written By John P. Kaufman

Boat Repair Made Easy — Finishes
Written By John P. Kaufman

Boat Repair Made Easy — Systems
Written By John P. Kaufman

Boat Repair Made Easy — Engines
Written By John P. Kaufman

Standard Ship's Log
Designed By John P. Kaufman

Large Ship's Log
Designed By John P. Kaufman

Custom Ship's Log
Designed By John P. Kaufman

Designing Power & Sail
Written By Arthur Edmunds

Fiberglass Boat Survey
Written By Arthur Edmunds

Building A Fiberglass Boat
Written By Arthur Edmunds

Buying A Great Boat
Written By Arthur Edmunds

Outfitting & Organizing Your Boat For A Day, A Week or A Lifetime
Written By Michael L. Frankel

Boater's Book of Nautical Terms
Written By David S. Yetman

Modern Boatworks
Written By David S. Yetman

Practical Seamanship
Written By David S. Yetman

Captain Jack's Basic Navigation
Written By Jack I. Davis

Captain Jack's Celestial Navigation
Written By Jack I. Davis

Captain Jack's Complete Navigation
Written By Jack I. Davis

Daddy & I Go Boating
Written By Ken Kreisler

My Grandpa Is A Tugboat Captain
Written By Ken Kreisler

Billy The Oysterman
Written By Ken Kreisler

Creating Comfort Afloat
Written By Janet Groene

Living Aboard
Written By Janet Groene

Simple Boat Projects
Written By Donald Boone

Racing The Ice To Cape Horn
Written By Frank Guernsey & Cy Zoerner

Boater's Checklist
Written By Clay Kelley

Florida Through The Islands What Boaters Need To Know
Written By Captain Clay Kelley & Marybeth

Marine Weather Forecasting
Written By J. Frank Brumbaugh

Basic Boat Maintenance
Written By J. Frank Brumbaugh

Complete Guide To Gasoline Marine Engines
Written By John Fleming

Complete Guide To Outboard Engines
Written By John Fleming

Complete Guide To Diesel Marine Engines
Written By John Fleming

Trouble Shooting Gasoline Marine Engines
Written By John Fleming

Trailer Boats
Written By Alex Zidock

Skipper's Handbook
Written By Robert S. Grossman

Wake Up & Water Ski
Written By Kimberly P. Robinson

White Squall - The Last Voyage Of Albatross
Written By Richard E. Langford

Cruising South
What to Expect Along The ICW
Written By Joan Healy

Electronics Aboard
Written By Stephen Fishman

A Whale At the Port Quarter
A Treasure Chest of Sea Stories
Written By Charles Gnaegy

Five Against The Sea
A True Story of Courage & Survival
Written By Ron Arias

Scuttlebutt
Seafaring History & Lore
Written By Captain John Guest USCG Ret.

Basic Boat Maintenance - - J. Frank Brumbaugh

Cruising The South Pacific
Written By Douglas Austin

After Forty Years
How To Avoid The Pitfalls of Boating
Written By David Wheeler

Catch of The Day
How To Catch, Clean & Cook It
Written By Carla Johnson

VHF Marine Radio Handbook
Written By Mike Whitehead

Basic Boat Maintenance - - *J. Frank Brumbaugh*

ABOUT THE AUTHOR

J. Frank Brumbaugh

After serving in Europe as a parachutist in the 82nd Airborne Division during WWII he became interested in small boats. As an Electronics Engineer he designed many electronic accessories for small boats including radio direction finders, depth sounders, fuel vapor alarms, battery charge meters, etc. with Heath Company. He has been awarded five U. S. Patents for electronic circuit designs.

Later his electronics work took him to Florida in 1959 where he sailed the Atlantic and Gulf of Mexico. During vacations he crewed on commercial fishing boats. His ability to translate "engineering speak" to simple sentences and his wish for more "down time" to go sailing convinced him to become a self-employed engineering consultant. During this period he wrote more than 50 technical books and numerous military Specifications and Standards for all branches of the military. Between contracts he took advantage of many sailing opportunities.

He has researched and written several books concerning his first love, boats. Drawing not only upon his long and varied experience but also those of many sailors he has interviewed over the years.

Frank has recently spent over five years living aboard and island hopping on his 25-foot Hunter, *Jade Lotus*. He continues to write for national magazines.

www.ingramcontent.com/pod-product-compliance
Lightning Source LLC
Chambersburg PA
CBHW031643170426
43195CB00035B/455